Information is Empowering
Developing Public Library Services
for Youth at Risk

SO-ECY-071

by Stan Weisner, Ph.D.
Director, Bay Area Youth at Risk Project

Second Edition
Edited by Katie Scarborough
Illustrated with photographs by Nita Winter

Bay Area Library and Information System
Oakland, California
1992
Funded by the Library Services and Construction Act

Publication of this guidebook was supported in part by the U.S. Department of Education, under the provisions of the Library Services and Construction Act, Title I, administered in California by the State Librarian. However, the opinions expressed herein do not necessarily reflect the position or policy of the U.S. Department of Education or the California State Library, and no official endorsement by the U.S. Department of Education or the California State Library should be inferred.

Photographs that appear in this guidebook were produced independently of the narrative and bear no direct relationship to concepts discussed in the text.

Printed on recycled paper

Information is Empowering: Developing Public Library Services for Youth at Risk

Table of Contents

Acknowledgements

The Bay Area Youth at Risk (YAR) Project was initiated by the Bay Area Library and Information System (BALIS), whose member libraries chose to become active partners in finding better ways to serve California's youth.

First and foremost, thanks to Ruth Foley Metz, System Coordinator for BALIS, for her leadership and guidance in initiating the project and making it come alive, as well as to the BALIS Administrative Council for its enduring support. Thanks are also due to:

- the California Library Services Board, who in 1988 established youth at risk as their next priority for CLSA funding, encouraging the California library field to develop more youth at risk programs;
- the YAR Project Advisory Committee members, especially Effie Lee Morris, who lent their names and seasoned advice to the overall community effort;
- the members of the YAR Project Steering Committee, chaired by Regina Minudri, Director of the Berkeley Public Library, and co-chaired by Adelia Lines, Director of the Richmond Public Library, for their critical advisory roles;
- the BALIS Children's Services Committee and especially its subcommittee members (Sherry Kumler, Julie Odofin, and Neel Parikh) who originated the request for the initial grant proposal and helped shape the overall project design;
- the local YAR team chairs from each library system and the willing community participants who served on each team;
- the hard-working research consultants who helped each YAR team collect and analyze needs assessment data;
- Jayne Becker, for developing materials used in the chapter on plan development and for her talent and success as a grantwriter for this project;
- Harder+Kibbe Research, for providing much of the material in the introduction to this edition and for their cogent evaluation of the YAR Project;
- the group of Oakland teens from St. Elizabeth's Youth Development Corporation who ably conducted their own library participant survey;
- the Urban Strategies Council which provided socio-demographic maps of the neighborhood around the Martin Luther King, Jr. Branch of the Oakland Public Library;
- the project's technical assistants, who included an unflappable accountant (Lee Montana) and creative editors and support staff (Merle Bachman, Jessi Bowen, Claudia Lunstroth, and Jane Walsh);
- Janet Hoffman, from the Bay Area Information and Retrieval System (BAIRS), for graciously agreeing to generate the sampling list for the project's youth provider survey;
- the BALIS System Advisory Board (SAB) for adopting youth at risk as its two-year priority, and to Gary Morrison for his invaluable assistance to the SAB as a BALIS staff intern;
- members of the BALIS Public Information Committee, who helped organize project publicity and media events; Atriom Productions for developing creative video materials and PSAs performed by a talented rap artist, Chill E. B.; and Sara Rosen, an Alameda County Young Adult librarian and local artist who helped design the project logo;
- the organization of Bay Area Young Adult librarians (BAYA), who provided both moral support and letters of support for the project;
- the many reviewers who read through early drafts of this guidebook and provided extremely helpful comments and suggestions;

- the California State Library, which funded the project through the Library Services and Construction Act (LSCA), and Gary Strong, California State Librarian; and special thanks to Bessie Egan, California State Library Children and Youth Consultant, who has been of great assistance in her role as project liaison and in her contributions to this book;
- the San Francisco Foundation for its generous supplemental support of the YAR pilot projects; and the Roberts Foundation for its funding of YAR Project T-shirts given to participating teens in all nine sites.

Finally, a special thank you to all the youth focus group participants and youth service providers who gave of their time to be interviewed and especially to all the Bay Area young adult librarians who on a daily basis put their own unfunded ideas and "pilot projects" to work, for the benefit of all youth who seek their help.

Bay Area Youth at Risk Project

Advisory Committee

Jose Arredondo	Spanish-Speaking Citizens Foundation
Angela Blackwell	Urban Strategies Council
Hon. Cathie Brown	Mayor, City of Livermore
David Carillo	The United Way (Contra Costa County)
Suzanne Calpestri	Library, University of California, Berkeley
Keith Choy	Mayor's Office of Children, Youth and Families (San Francisco)
Deborah Ellwood	Children Now
Effie Lee Morris	California Library Services Board
Hon. Don Perata	Alameda County Board of Supervisors
Gail Steele	Eden Youth Center (Hayward)
Paul Anderson/Clare Stich	Bay Area Young Adult Librarians
Peder Thoreen	Youth Representative, National White House Conference on Libraries and Information Services
Alan Watahara	Children and Youth Policy Project
Professor Judith Weedman	School of Library and Information Studies, University of California, Berkeley
Sylvia Yee	San Francisco Foundation

Steering Committee Participants

Alameda County Library	Caryn Sipos/Judy Flum/Gary Morrison
Alameda Free Library	Jane Chisaki
Berkeley Public Library	Regina Minudri/Kay Finney
Contra Costa County Library	Janet Hildebrand/Susan Reeve/Stella Baker/Linda Phillips
Hayward Public Library	Sherry Kumler
Livermore Public Library	Julie Casamajor
Oakland Public Library	Julie Odofin/Garrett Lambrev
Richmond Public Library	Adelia Lines/Emma Clark/Angela Cox/Tarnel Abbott
San Francisco Public Library	Neel Parikh/Toni Bernardi/Lee Olivier/Thomas Tavis
California State Library	Bessie Egan

The Purpose of This Guidebook

This guidebook offers public librarians ideas and techniques to better serve teenagers in their communities. It is based on two assumptions. First, young adults in the United States today are increasingly at risk of a broad range of social and economic problems. Second, with training, administrative support and effective involvement of the community, public librarians can expand their role in serving this increasingly vulnerable population. It is our goal to help libraries become key partners in improving services to at-risk youth in communities throughout the country.

The goals of the guidebook are threefold:
- To inform and inspire public librarians to respond to the growing needs of families, especially those with at-risk teenagers
- To compile a useful, readable manual that documents the experience of the YAR Project in the San Francisco Bay Area
- To provide a practical guide that can be used by other libraries and library systems to train their staffs to expand and improve public library services to at-risk teens in their communities

The book begins with an introduction that outlines how libraries in the San Francisco Bay Area improved services to at-risk youth during the Bay Area Youth at Risk (YAR) Project. The two-year (1990-1992) YAR Project was sponsored by the Bay Area Library and Information System (BALIS) and funded by the California State Library through the Library Services and Construction Act (LSCA). In its second year, it received supplemental funding from the San Francisco Foundation to support YAR pilot projects in each library system. A timeline of key phases in the project is included in Appendix A.

The three counties served by BALIS — Alameda, Contra Costa and San Francisco — are home to a quarter million teens, ages twelve to eighteen. Like young people everywhere in the United States, these teenagers are suffering dramatically high rates of school failure, substance abuse and teen pregnancy; many of them are the victims of poverty and family violence. By participating in the YAR Project, each of the nine public library systems in BALIS hoped to improve their ability to respond to the pressing needs of these at-risk youth.

In evaluating the YAR Project, consultants at San Francisco-based Harder+Kibbe Research helped identify six basic approaches to youth services taken by the participating BALIS libraries. The models outlined in the introduction are Harder+Kibbe's descriptions of these approaches for providing library services to at-risk youth. Some models, such as Young Adult Collection and Facility Development, fit easily into the traditional pattern of service offered by libraries. Others, such as Programs for Youth, can be more innovative and require additional effort and/or resources from the library and librarians. As the consultants are quick to point out, however, what seems easiest for libraries is often least effective at serving the target population.

Against the background of the projects and models described in the introduction, the remainder of this book provides step-by-step guidance to establishing and/or improving services to at-risk youth in any public library. The chapters of the book start with the first steps of the process of developing public library services for at-risk youth — assessing need, pursuing community outreach, training, and planning — and end with a discussion of proposal writing, program evaluation, effective use of the media, and child/youth advocacy. Each chapter contains a brief discussion of the issue outlining a step-by-step methodology, followed by a case example based on BALIS YAR Project experiences and a selection of practical exercises.

Much of the material covered in this guidebook is applicable to developing programs for any underserved population. In fact, some of the material draws from resources developed for previous California State Library programs (e.g., Partnerships for Change, Family Literacy). Each section focuses on the role of the public librarian and uses examples directly related to needs of at-risk youth.

The guidebook does not cover specialized topics related to Young Adult (YA) collection development or how to set up a teen corner in a library (a few books covering such topics are referenced in the bibliography). Its primary focus is on the process involved in creating and developing new library services for at-risk teens in the broader community context. It highlights topics not generally covered in most graduate library programs.

As is often the case, the long-range impact of the ideas discussed in this book ultimately depends on the leadership and commitment of library management, whose on-going support remains critical for any substantive, programmatic efforts to expand and improve YA services. Libraries must be willing to provide physical space in the library and sustained staffing and programming support for teen services once initial needs assessment, planning, and outreach efforts have been completed.

The development of visible and successful programs by BALIS public libraries targeting at-risk youth was well received by the general public and San Francisco Bay Area media. It is hoped that such efforts will continue here and in addition, be established in other parts of the country. At the same time, we can urge policymakers who determine budget priorities at the national, state and local levels to more actively support public libraries and the key role they can play in the lives of our nation's most valuable resource — its children and youth.

"Use this manual to make something happen for the kids in your community."

— *BALIS YAR Project administrator*

Definition of Terms

This book uses terminology drawn from the world of young adults and young adult librarianship as well as that of library services planning. Some practitioners may feel fluent in these languages already. For those who are not, a brief review of this section before reading on will contribute to a better understanding of terms used throughout this book.

At-risk youth

See **Youth at risk**

CBO

Abbreviation for community-based organization.

Child/youth advocacy organization

A public or non-profit organization whose primary purpose is to speak out or write in support of the needs of children and youth. There are legislative, judicial and administrative advocates for children and youth which operate on the local, state, national, and international level.

Community-based organization

A private, non-profit organization which has a board of directors and receives funding from fees for service, government contracts, United Way, corporate and foundation donations, etc. Abbreviated: **CBO**.

Community involvement

A process of including various community groups and individuals in the planning, development and delivery of library services and programming.

Community outreach

A strategy for making library services more accessible using publicity, off-site service delivery, and the development of library linkages and coalitions with community-based organizations.

Consultant

An individual with specific skills or expertise, usually hired on a contractual basis to give professional or expert advice on a project. A consultant may provide a library with skills not available in-house, or may simply be someone with similar skills to library staff but more time to devote to a project.

Evaluation

A research strategy aimed at assessing the activities and outcomes of a specific program. It includes both process (what happened) and outcome (program results and impacts) measures of success.

Interagency collaboration

Formal cooperation or partnerships between agencies serving the same population. Collaborative strategies can include: joint planning and fundraising, placing programs on existing sites (e.g., schools, recreation centers, libraries), developing partnerships which include co-locating services on common sites (e.g., multi-service teen centers).

Multicultural services	A programmatic response to the cultural and ethnic diversity in a community requiring a basic knowledge, sensitivity and awareness of other cultural groups.
Request for proposal	A formal statement by a funder soliciting applications by eligible agencies and/or individuals to deliver a service to a target population. Abbreviated: **RFP**.
Research design	A plan to conduct research which responds to specific questions and describes how the researcher is going to collect and analyze data to answer those questions.
Teen	See **Young adult**
YA	Abbreviation for young adult.
YAR	Abbreviation for youth at risk.
Young adult	Defined by libraries as a person age twelve to eighteen; used interchangeably in this book with the term "teen." Abbreviated: **YA**.
Young adult services	Traditional library services provided by public libraries aimed mostly at teens.
Youth at risk	Adolescents whose potential of becoming healthy and productive adults is reduced because they are at high risk of encountering serious problems at home, in school, or in their communities. Youth at risk for the Bay Area YAR Project included adolescents who were most likely to engage or had engaged in "risk-taking behaviors" (see Irwin, 1990), but its primary focus was on youth ages twelve to eighteen who were at high or moderately high levels of risk. Abbreviated: **YAR**.
Youth needs assessment	A study or assessment to identify the individual needs of youth — from the very basic (food, clothing, and shelter) to higher level needs including education, recreation and nurturing — and gauge the degree to which they are being met.
Youth-serving network	The formal and informal system which helps to meet the needs of adolescents and their families in the community (e.g., government and non-profit clinics, agencies, programs, clubs, etc., as well as the local education system).
Youth service agency	A public, non-profit, or for-profit organization whose target population is primarily adolescents. Examples include: teen health/mental health clinics, adolescent drug treatment/prevention programs, recreation centers, YMCAs/YWCAs, homeless youth programs, and summer youth employment programs.

INTRODUCTION:

San Francisco Bay Area Libraries and Their Ideas for Serving At-Risk Teens

In 1990, the California State Library awarded a Library Services and Construction Act (LSCA) grant to the Bay Area Library and Information System (BALIS) to conduct a needs assessment and implement plans for services to youth at risk in its member libraries. BALIS, one of California's fifteen cooperative library systems, is an organization of nine public libraries in three counties of the San Francisco Bay Area. By pursuing this project, the system set out to plan and develop programs for teens not in isolation, but as part of a community-wide response to youth at risk.

With BALIS' help during the planning year, the nine member libraries conducted community needs assessments with young adults ages twelve to eighteen and with local youth-serving community agencies, and developed plans to increase library services to meet priority needs. Hundreds of Bay Area youth service providers and teenagers were interviewed and surveyed in the nine sites during the Bay Area Youth at Risk Project needs assessment process.

There was a general consensus among those contacted that libraries are an invaluable resource for teenagers and that librarians need to be more actively involved in responding to the growing needs of at-risk youth. While libraries may not be viewed as the lead agency in addressing many of the most serious social problems highlighted in the YAR needs assessment process — substance abuse, teen pregnancy, and gang violence, for example — they are perceived as a new and invaluable neighborhood-based partner for youth-serving agencies on the "front line."

Strategies developed during the planning process for local libraries to expand and improve services to at-risk youth reflected priorities identified during this needs assessment phase of the project. At each library, the needs assessment process (described in detail in Chapter I) involved a local YAR planning team composed of both library and community participants. Teams helped make recommendations for YA services based on data collected from youth focus groups, existing statistical reports, a mailed survey, and interviews with youth service providers.

Nine Youth at Risk Pilot Projects

Plans for YAR pilot projects developed by each of the nine libraries were implemented during the second year of the YAR Project. They are summarized below.

Alameda County Library

Within the Alameda County Library system, the San Lorenzo Branch conducted a pilot program to serve 3,000 teens in the unincorporated areas near San Lorenzo, including regular outreach programs at local high schools designed to familiarize students with the informational and recreational resources available at the library. In San Lorenzo, the major identified need was for information directly related to jobs and job skills, multicultural relations, health and sexuality.

In response, the San Lorenzo Branch, along with other community agencies, held a series of six teen forums on these key issues. The library also distributed a resource guide for youth, held a "Stump the Librarian" contest at the local high school as a youth outreach vehicle, gave books to a continuation school, conducted a youth panel discussion, and held regular local YAR steering committee meetings.

The project reached over 400 youth through the "Stump the Librarian" contest, which was followed up with in-house activities as well as the youth forums. The contest gave the library a great deal of exposure and appeared to make youth feel more comfortable about using the library. During the grant period, YA circulation increased by thirty percent.

Alameda Free Library

Responding to an overriding concern among the City of Alameda's 5,000 teens about doing well in school, the Alameda Free Library planned to act as a clearinghouse for tutors who provide homework support. In addition, since Alameda's needs assessment revealed a general lack of awareness of the resources of the library and other youth service providers, the library decided to increase publicity to young audiences by distributing bookcovers, improve access to teen materials by improving the teen area, compile a youth services directory, and improve communication and coordination of services with other youth-serving agencies.

The library's primary success was in printing and distributing a large amount of material which directly relates to teens. Five thousand bookcovers were printed and distributed through middle and high schools. Three thousand hip-pocket guides to youth services were printed and distributed through the library. A new, larger YA space was also established in the library.

Because there were more students wishing to use the tutoring clearinghouse than tutors — who were to come from sources outside the library — staff was unable to initiate the tutoring clearinghouse before the close of the YAR grant period. The library hopes to pursue this program in the future, as well as to increase spending for teen materials if the city budget allows.

Berkeley Public Library

In Berkeley, the library discovered that employment among African American and Hispanic young people was the greatest unmet need, and that, as in other jurisdictions, many of Berkeley's 7,000 teens were unaware of resources offered by the library. The Berkeley Public Library decided to hire teens to conduct an outreach campaign among their peers to raise their awareness of library and community services.

Three teens were hired as employees, and two remained through the grant period. Berkeley Public Library planned to implement permanent, part-time jobs for youth at risk in January, 1993. in addition, a youth rap and poetry program was held at the central library. The library had hoped to produce additional programs but logistics and staff time limitations prevented this. The library also improved the YA collections by purchasing videos dealing with health and mental health issues.

In August, 1992, the library conducted an all staff workshop on awareness of the problems, attitudes and needs of at-risk youth. Many teens participated in small group discussions on youth at risk.

Contra Costa County Library

Serving 63,000 teens, the Contra Costa County Library found a lack of information on youth services, a lack of coordination among the area's youth-serving agencies, and a lack of outreach by the library to the agencies. Accordingly, the library decided to build a collection of video and print "discussion starter" materials and promote its use by organizations and individuals who serve young adults, particularly in the San Pablo area. To improve outreach and aid coordination among youth-serving agencies, the San Pablo Branch worked with neighboring Richmond Public Library to co-host quarterly meetings of community-based organizations (CBOs) serving at-risk youth. Participation in these meetings grew from eight to sixty organizations during the course of the YAR grant period (also see Richmond Public Library, below).

The San Pablo Branch also targeted a junior high school Asian youth group for programs on homework help, library access skills and multicultural awareness. Outreach to at-risk youth was most broadly accomplished with the library's production and distribution of a hip-pocket teen resource guide, referring youth to agencies which could provide direct assistance with crisis issues. Three guides were produced for West, East and Central Contra Costa County, with collaboration from Richmond Public Library in production of the West County guide.

Hayward Public Library

The major needs identified for Hayward's 9,000 young adults were school drop-out prevention and increased access to neighborhood-based services which help with obstacles faced in daily life. In response to those needs, the Hayward Public Library decided to provide speakers in neighborhood settings on practical topics such as finding and holding a job or staying free of drugs. The library ultimately held one program, "Let's Talk About Sex," rated ten on a scale of one to ten by nine of the fifteen teens attending. The library plans to hold additional forums in the future.

In addition, the library created an up-to-date resource file of pamphlets on relevant topics for distribution to teens. The library also widely distributed a hip-pocket resource guide prepared by the Southern Alameda County Network of Youth Services.

Livermore Public Library

Success in school was the overwhelming priority of Livermore's 5,000 teens. Older youth were concerned about future employment, while younger teens were challenged by peer relationships. Many teens were unaware of or were discontented with library services, particularly with the requirement that persons under eighteen needed a parent's signature to obtain a library card. The YAR Project resulted in the review of this requirement, and the library decided to allow anyone sixteen or older with identification to receive a card.

The Livermore Public Library also worked with other agencies to produce a booklet — entitled *Under 18 and Unhappy At Home?* — about services and options for youth in difficult situations. The booklet serves as a troubleshooting guide, listing potential teen problems and solutions with contact information for appropriate service agencies. In the first five months it was available, the library distributed 2,500 copies at the library itself, through local service providers, and through high schools.

The library increased programs on finding jobs and developing interviewing skills, held workshops on vocational opportunities after high school, and expanded its hiring of young people as library aides and pages. Improved outreach programs concentrated on educating teens about the Young Adult area, library circulation policies and library access skills. A video about library on-line computer use was put into production during the grant period, and 4,000 bookmarks were printed and distributed at local high schools and through the Livermore Area Recreation and Park District. The library also added to its collection of nonfiction for young adults.

Oakland Public Library

Dropping out of school and below-grade literacy levels were among the most serious problems faced by the 31,000 teenagers in Oakland. In response, the library created an after school tutoring/homework center at the Martin Luther King, Jr. Branch in East Oakland to help young adults improve study skills and master school assignments. The program was designed to serve twelve to fifteen year olds who attend the six middle, junior high or high schools in the vicinity. The library recruited additional tutors to supplement those currently working in youth agency tutoring programs. Approximately 130 youths between the ages of ten and fifteen signed up for the program during the grant period. Saturday morning tutoring proved to be the most successful portion of the program, with volunteer tutors more consistently available at that time than during the week.

The library also held a program, "The Politics of Rap," which was attended by over 200 people, primarily teens. The event, hosted by a local disc jockey, included both informative discussion and rap music performances.

Richmond Public Library

Low literacy skills and a high drop-out rate among Richmond's 7,700 young people were the primary needs identified by the Richmond Public Library. The library's new Tutoring Library Connection service planned to support the tutoring programs currently provided by community-based organizations (CBOs) by offering materials and speakers to augment these programs. The library contacted two CBOs, visited each with its Mobile Outreach Program van, participated in programs with each group, and handed out books supportive of studying and homework.

In addition, the Richmond Public Library disseminated a hip-pocket resource guide to youth services, published in collaboration with the Contra Costa County Library. Richmond also cooperated with the San Pablo Branch of the Contra Costa County Library in holding forums for area CBOs (also see Contra Costa County Library, above). The library created a tutor referral list and publicized its tutoring outreach at a district career fair.

San Francisco Public Library

A needs assessment of San Francisco's 45,000 teens revealed that middle school youth from African American, Latino and limited English speaking populations had great difficulty in accessing information to assist in dealing with poverty, education, health, discrimination and newcomer adjustment. To respond, San Francisco Public Library established a Teen Corner with an expanded collection at its Bayview-Anna E. Waden Branch in the Bayview/Hunters Point neighborhood. The branch also hoped to work with three community agencies to develop cooperative projects serving Bayview/Hunters Point teens.

Patterns for library services of off-site and deposit collections were explored by establishing library services at the Youth Guidance Center (Juvenile Hall). Services included weekly visits to bring fiction and nonfiction books as well as popular magazines to the multiethnic, multilingual residents of the Youth Guidance Center.

Models for Service to Youth at Risk

During the second year of the YAR grant period, the programs described above were evaluated by the San Francisco consulting firm of Harder+Kibbe Research. In the process of their evaluation, it became clear that the YAR activities pursued by the BALIS libraries fell into a limited number of categories. These categories of activity represent models for library response to youth at risk. They are alike in that they follow certain sequences of progression and use similar methods to achieve an outcome.

The models outlined by Harder+Kibbe, described below, are not mutually exclusive; several of the BALIS libraries have pursued more than one simultaneously. However, they do represent distinct approaches to making libraries more responsive to youth at risk. Libraries interested in increasing their ability to serve youth at risk can look to these models as examples of what others have attempted.

A library's choice of a model or models should be based on the consideration of two factors: the needs of youth and the capacity of the library system. While all the models described below will certainly provide some benefit to young people, their benefit can be enhanced if they relate directly to the needs of local youth. The model selected should also fit into the broader youth-serving context of the community.

Model #1: Providing information about services

For many young people, the array of services available to them can be daunting and can sometimes discourage them from getting needed help. Some services are provided by public agencies (e.g., schools, police and probation departments, clinics, recreation departments), some by private agencies (e.g., youth service agencies, family counseling, alcohol and drug treatment services) and some have no formal agency auspice at all (e.g., churches and sports organizations). In some areas, the overlapping jurisdictions of public agencies can add to the confusion.

These factors highlight the need among youth for basic information about services in their community. Most of the BALIS libraries used this model as part of their YAR program. They explicitly identified a lack of information as a need and developed products — booklets, hip-pocket guides to youth services, informational bookcovers and bookmarks — to meet that need. Some libraries chose to provide simple listings of services, while others provided more detailed information. Livermore Public Library, for example, produced the booklet *Under 18 and Unhappy at Home?*, which gives teens alternative solutions to particular problems, tells them who to contact for help, and explains how particular agencies will respond to their requests.

An assumption that underlies this model is that of the library as "third party" acting as intermediary between youth at risk and other community resources. For many vulnerable youth, the library is not one of the youth-serving organizations they would choose to use first, if at all. Guides to community resources are more likely to facilitate the use of non-library agencies. This is consistent with the traditional library mission of providing information. It is not likely to increase library use or raise awareness of the library among youth at risk.

Model #2: Young adult collection and facility development

One of the most common models used in the BALIS projects was enhancement of the libraries' existing capacity to serve young people. The collection development activities focused on acquiring books, periodicals, videos and music (tapes and compact disks) with a young adult emphasis. In addition, funds were used to purchase video equipment for use by young adult library users and by youth-serving agencies in local communities.

Related to this is facility development. Several BALIS libraries used YAR Project funds to improve their YA space. They upgraded signage as well as purchasing new shelving and furniture.

As with the development of youth resource guides, this is a relatively easy model to implement. However, its effectiveness in reaching youth at risk is open to question. This model is most likely to benefit existing young library users who want more materials targeted specially to their needs or who would appreciate their own space. It is possible that by expanding the range of books, periodicals, recordings or videos a library may encourage young people who have not been users to access the library. Once they have come in, they may find other materials that may be helpful to them.

Model #3: Programs for youth

An innovative model for serving youth at risk is the provision of special programs for them. These programs typically do not have a library focus — they do not directly include or promote the library. Instead, the library offers something of value and interest to young people and in the process raises its visibility. This in turn reduces youth resistance to the library, changing perceptions of the library from that of a "boring" place with an academic focus to that of a more vital and engaging setting. Holding these programs at the library can further increase the comfort level of young people with the institution.

"This didn't happen as I expected, but it's turning out great. I think almost every kid here will come back to the library sometime."

— *library staff member after Politics of Rap event, Oakland Public Library*

Program topics at BALIS libraries covered a wide range, from jobs and sex to rap and poetry. These topics were of general interest to teens but may have been of particular interest to those without significant academic interests. Of special concern to youth in the Bay Area were topics relating to cultural or ethnic diversity.

Generally, the programs involved individuals from outside the library, although library staff were present. Where there was a body of knowledge to be conveyed, as in Hayward Public Library's "Let's Talk About Sex" program or Alameda County Library's employment workshop in San Lorenzo, knowledgeable people from community agencies provided the expertise. Several of the programs focused on youth culture and involved rappers and poets.

Special programs for youth with non-traditional topics represent a promising model for reaching youth at risk. If the publicity for the programs can be targeted to hard-to-reach youth, they can provide useful information and introduce the library as a source of additional help. A seemingly minor but sometimes significant factor is logistics. The schedules of teenagers are more complex than many adults expect. Several BALIS libraries assumed that events would be well-attended and found, to their chagrin, that the target audience had other plans. Friday nights are not opportune times for scheduling events.

Model #4: Tutoring programs

A fourth model for serving youth at risk is to provide assistance that will enhance academic performance. In the BALIS YAR Project, such assistance took the form of tutoring. Tutoring is the process of providing help with academic subjects outside of the school setting. Two variations of this model were pursued in this effort. Under the first variation, the library organized and operated the tutoring program, as was done at the Martin Luther King, Jr. Branch of the Oakland Public Library. This entailed recruiting tutors, enrolling students, scheduling sessions and providing tutoring space.

In two of the other sites, the libraries planned to act as clearing-houses for tutoring help. The Richmond Public and Alameda Free libraries intended to put together a directory of community tutoring resources and then refer interested young people to the appropriate agency. In Alameda, there was considerable student interest in seeking tutors, but the library was unable to locate an adequate supply of people. In Richmond, the YA librarian compiled a two-page list of tutoring sources. Richmond focused on supporting extant tutoring programs offered by CBOs. Librarians visited the tutoring sites, gave instruction on library use and handed out books supportive of studying and homework.

Tutoring is a difficult model to implement. If a library offers its own tutoring program, it must coordinate the schedules of a number of individuals. Unless the library can assure students that there will be an adequate supply of tutors and vice versa, enthusiasm for the program may wane. Finding the overlap between the schedules of volunteer tutors and students may be difficult.

Libraries performing a clearinghouse function can only be as effective as the resources to which they refer. Student interest appears to be high for such referrals.

Model #5: Community outreach

The community outreach model involves taking library resources out of their traditional setting and placing them directly in the community. This can involve working with community-based organizations which serve youth or by involving the library in community activities without the auspices of a community agency. In some instances in the BALIS YAR Project, library staff have almost "exported" the library to community groups. This was the case in Richmond, where the Mobile Outreach Program van took a selection of young adult reading material to community organizations, and San Francisco, where community outreach took the form of library visits to the Youth Guidance Center (YGC), San Francisco's Juvenile Hall.

The San Francisco program identified a group of youth who were at very high risk of continuing to get in trouble. They were already in the juvenile justice system and, for many of them, the progression to adult crimes would be a natural one. By making library resources and the careful attention of an adult available to them, the YAR Project offered the possibility that they might avoid future incarceration.

A different variation of the community outreach model was undertaken by the Alameda County Library's San Lorenzo Branch. Here the target group was the entire student body of a public high school. The library staff engaged the school in a "Stump the Librarian" contest that attracted a great deal of attention and promoted the library.

These two successful examples show that community outreach can be an effective way to access youth who might otherwise never come into the library. The San Francisco experience with the YGC, however, suggests that it takes a great deal of time to build relationships with service providers. The YGC program was able to begin only after six months of planning and coordination. Other libraries had similar experiences. While many youth-serving agencies may express a willingness to incorporate library services into what they already offer youth, making the actual arrangements can be very time-consuming and may not always end in success.

Model #6: Integrating youth into the library

The sixth model evidenced in the BALIS YAR Project is that of integrating youth into the library. In this model, representatives of the population to be reached by the library become involved in the library's work. This happened in two distinct ways in BALIS libraries. The first was the Young Adult Consultants (YACs) to the San Lorenzo Branch of the Alameda County Library. The YACs are youths (typically high school students) who advise the branch about YA materials, programs, and other activities, essentially serving as a teen council or youth advisory group. They play an active role in setting the direction of the Young Adult program in San Lorenzo.

Another approach is the one taken by the Berkeley Public Library, which works with its own Young Adult Advisory Committee (YAAC). In Berkeley, the library hired high school students from the community with the expectation that they would assist in planning YAR programs as well as perform routine library functions. The most' difficult aspect of this plan was the administrative inconvenience of trying to get these hires through the City of Berkeley's personnel process. Although the process was laborious, the library believes it has been successful and hopes eventually to be able to hire up to fifteen high school students. Interviews with the youth themselves revealed they were pleased to have the jobs.

These experiences in Berkeley and San Lorenzo showed that young adults have much to offer the library. Budget is required to hire youth as library employees but the costs of forming a youth advisory group are minimal. All that is required for the advisory group is library staff enthusiastic enough to keep young people participating actively. Either strategy will help to ensure that the perspective of young people is represented in any planning related to YAR activities.

Ideas for Teen Library Services

There are many specific YA program ideas being implemented in BALIS libraries, especially in the Alameda County and Berkeley Public Library systems which have YA designated staff, that are not necessarily reflected in the projects described above. While this guidebook is not meant as a comprehensive resource for teen library activities, the list below — generated by participants at a YAR Project training session — will give the reader some practical ideas for possible approaches to YA program development.

The physical layout:
- Designate a teen corner.
- Use bright and colorful signs.
- Put up age-appropriate posters.
- Use more comfortable furniture.
- Put up a bulletin board.
- Develop a listening center (CDs, tapes).

Collection development/materials:

- Review and update the book and paperback collection (see Boegen, 1986, for current list of YA titles).
- Develop non-English materials as needed.
- Display popular and current magazines/newspapers.
- Update the CD/tape collection.
- Keep a current teen resource pamphlet file on services/programs.
- Highlight career/college materials.
- Collect up-to-date materials on topical issues (AIDS, cultural heros, teen pregnancy, etc.).

School/library coordination:

- Develop contacts with local schools.
- Publicize special library events for teens.
- Request "homework alert" notices from teachers before library assignment are made.
- Schedule booktalks and other programs at local schools.

Community outreach:

- Contact local youth-serving agencies and exchange information on services for teens.
- Visit special programs for teens (juvenile hall, recreation centers, group homes, etc.).
- Develop collaborative programs with local agencies.
- Create an active youth advisory committee.
- Set up special community-based programs where teens hang out (shopping malls, YMCA/YWCA, playgrounds, etc.).

Special programs:

- Organize and publicize teen summer reading programs (with prizes).
- Expand multicultural programming for teens and their families.
- Create special programs for teens (rap/poetry sessions, teen forums, speakers, etc.).
- Develop regular teen programs in the library (summer reading programs, annual job fairs, tutoring/homework help centers, etc.).
- Invite teen "celebrities" to appear at library branches.
- Hire teens as peer tutors, pages, outreach workers, etc.

Child/youth advocacy:

- Create a staff development training component on YA issues.
- Support development of YA staff expertise.
- Insist on YA staff representation on the library management team.
- Work together with other child/youth advocates in the community to improve services.

The Importance of Planning

The chapters of this book explore aspects of the planning process most relevant to developing services to youth at risk. To some extent the organization of these planning steps into different chapters is artificial, since the stages of planning are interrelated and could take place in a number of different sequences depending on a library's circumstances.

Those familiar with the Public Library Development Project (PLDP) or other planning literature will recognize the parallels between steps and/or terms in this book and those described in *Planning and Role Setting for Public Libraries*. The latter book points out that planning can take place at various levels of effort. The library needn't avoid planning altogether if faced with limited resources, for example. Instead, by selecting a particular level of effort, a library can adapt the planning process to its own resources, needs, and goals. Whatever level of effort is chosen, the results can be valuable for the library.

Planning and Role Setting for Public Libraries defines three levels of effort for each planning task: basic, moderate and extensive. The level selected by the library will depend upon the number of participants in the process, the library's budget, the type of community, the purpose of planning, the formality or informality of planning procedures chosen, and the timeline.

The planning and needs assessment process was an integral part of the BALIS Youth at Risk Project, and the nature of the project was such that libraries generally pursued planning activities at the extensive level. Throughout this guidebook, case study examples are given of specific projects carried out by BALIS libraries. If a few of these projects seem elaborate or more extensive than you might select or design for your own library, keep in mind that the same general goals can be accomplished at lower levels of effort.

This book does not intend to chart a single path to providing services to youth at risk or planning services for youth at risk. Other planning methods are equally as valid, and any process which includes the basic planning components outlined here and in PLDP publications can work. But to ensure successful services that are responsive to the community, especially in times when resources are limited, it is important to engage in *some* systematic planning process.

It is important, also, to "plan to plan." This preparation phase sets the stage for all subsequent activities in the planning process. Especially by establishing a specific purpose for planning a library can give itself a guideline for its future planning decisions. Addressing preliminaries such as setting a schedule, allocating resources and identifying participants will give the library a clear picture of its planning context.

Additional information can be found in the PLDP planning manuals, including *Planning and Role Setting for Public Libraries* and *Output Measures for Public Libraries*. These and other planning manuals can be used in conjunction with this guidebook to help establish services for youth at risk. By drawing on these resources, a librarian increases the chances of creating and sustaining a strong YA program in collaboration with other youth-serving organizations and the community at large.

CHAPTER I

Youth Needs Assessment

A youth needs assessment is a community process and a means of gathering information about teenagers. Its primary goal is to identify the met and unmet needs of the population studied. A youth needs assessment provides a relatively objective basis from which a librarian can make more informed policy and program decisions to shape innovative teen services to address unmet needs of youth in specific communities. A youth needs assessment process should be thought of as an essential component of library service development.

Before a library develops or improves services for youth, it must find a way to meaningfully involve those who will be affected by the change: teens and youth service providers in the community. To best assess needs and plan for services, the library must involve appropriate members of the community as it determines its role. It must also find objective methods of identifying priority needs and filling service gaps which are based on a community consensus. Building that consensus is an essential ingredient in a successful youth needs assessment process.

WHY do a youth needs assessment

- To identify existing services and unmet needs
- To provide a basis for prioritizing needs and developing a library service plan for youth
- To engage other community-based organizations in helping to develop the library service plan for youth
- To provide initial service utilization and needs data that can be used to assess the impact of programs over time
- To raise community awareness of the growing needs of at-risk youth and, if appropriate, encourage other community organizations to work collaboratively on the issue

WHAT a librarian should do to conduct a youth needs assessment

Create a community process
- Involve key community leaders, community-based organizations, and youth representatives.
- Convene a forum at which these representatives can help shape the needs assessment process

Develop a realistic workplan and timetable
- Plan the scope of the work to focus on the most useful information the library needs to know about specific at-risk youth population(s).
- Plan the needs assessment process carefully, taking into account staff time and resource constraints.
- Retain the services of an outside consultant if needed.

Select an appropriate research design
- Develop a research design that draws on existing secondary data as well as primary data collected from youth and youth-service providers.
- Determine appropriate methods to gather primary data, including interviews, questionnaires and/or group interviews or focus groups.

HOW to do a youth needs assessment

An effective youth needs assessment is a community process that involves library staff, the network of youth-serving agencies and the youth themselves. The first step is to identify a target population (e.g., all teens ages twelve to eighteen within one library service area). Next, library staff should develop a realistic workplan that will earn the confidence and support of potential participants and the broader community. Finally, library staff, assisted by a consultant if needed, should fashion a research design that will generate useable information and answer the major questions posed by the study.

If the library chooses to retain the services of an outside consultant, library staff should still remain closely involved in the process. A research consultant should be retained who has a track record in the area of needs assessment and youth services and is willing to work within the existing time and budget constraints of the proposed study. In most cases, library staff needs to clearly define the scope of work to be done and work with the consultant to ensure a good research design. It is important to select a consultant who will both complement the skills of in-house library expertise and be able to work effectively with library staff and the community being studied.

In a case like that above, the library may hire a consultant in order to gain special expertise. In other cases, an outside consultant may not necessarily be someone who has more expertise than existing library staff. A consultant may simply be someone with more undivided time to devote to the needs assessment process. For example, most library staff will have writing skills, but may not have the blocks of time required to write a needs assessment report. Hiring a writing consultant can then supplement limited staff time and lend objectivity to the library's process.

Create a community process

Community involvement and shared ownership of the needs assessment process is crucial to the success of the project. Thus, library staff must assemble a team which represents a variety of backgrounds and reflects the community served by the library. In this way, the needs assessment process will gain community support and draw on the experience of those outside the library to help interpret the data collected and recommend feasible, effective responses to the identified needs.

Composition of the needs assessment team may overlap with that of the project advisory committee, depending on community circumstances and the library's goals (see Chapter III, "Establishing an Advisory Committee"). In any case, participants should include youth representatives, parents, public and non-profit youth-service providers and reflect the ethnic and cultural diversity of the community served (see sample team roster in Appendix B).

Examples of participants include the following:
- Youth representatives from local junior high and high schools
- Non-profit sector youth-service providers (YMCA/YWCA, Boys and Girls Club, residential or out-patient adolescent mental health or substance abuse program, etc.)
- Public sector youth-service providers (recreation, child welfare, police, juvenile justice, etc.)
- School representatives (school librarian, teacher or counselor)
- Business/corporate representatives (Chamber of Commerce, neighborhood business association)
- Elected officials or aides
- Parent activists or child/youth advocates (PTA president or advocacy group staff)
- Local university, college, or continuing education representatives
- Leaders of local ethnic organizations representative of the target population

In all cases, members should have these qualifications:
- knowledge of youth-related issues
- commitment to the issues of youth at risk
- willingness to give their time and expertise

To allow for adequate discussion at meetings, the team should be limited to twelve to fifteen members. After library staff has contacted them by phone or met with them in person to explain the purpose of the needs assessment, they should be formally invited by letter to participate.

Meetings should be held on a regular basis for a set period of time. Agendas should facilitate consensus on each of the key phases of the project:
- Defining the scope of the problem
- Setting team goals, objectives, and timelines
- Assigning tasks and responsibilities

- Designing the study
- Collecting and reviewing the data
- Interpreting the data and setting priorities for action
- Making recommendations for policy change and/or program development
- Disseminating findings
- Evaluating program development efforts

Organizing and running a successful and well-attended community meeting requires considerable pre-meeting preparation. Ideas on how to plan and run a productive meeting are covered in Chapter III, "Establishing an Advisory Committee."

The workplan and timetable

The workplan for the needs assessment study must define a realistic scope of work to be accomplished in a reasonable time-frame given available resources. The written workplan should include the assignment of paid or volunteer staff responsible for each task by a specified time.

The scope of work can be carefully circumscribed or broadly defined. Study questions can range from "How does the public library serve all at-risk youth in a diverse county?" to more manageable questions like "How could one neighborhood branch better serve the needs of early adolescent girls?" or "Which public library do you use and how often?" The breadth of questions asked in the needs assessment study will have much to do with the time and resources required to complete the project.

A needs assessment can be conducted in a few weeks or take up to a year, but a reasonable time period is three to six months. A timeline for a six-month needs assessment process is suggested in Figure 1.

Figure 1. Needs Assessment Timeline

Month	1	2	3	4	5	6
Defining scope of work	▓					
Recruiting advisory team	▓					
Hiring research staff (optional)		▓				
Reviewing existing reports/studies	▓	▓				
Designing needs assessment		▓				
Collecting data		▓	▓			
Analyzing findings				▓		
Writing report					▓	
Disseminating results						▓

Decisions on timing and the scope of work are almost totally dependent on the availability of in-kind library staff time and funding for the study. Even with a modest budget of $2,000 to $3,000, library staff can hire a part-time research consultant (and/or faculty/graduate student expertise from a nearby college or university) for the following sort of assistance:

- Help in designing the study
- Assistance with data analysis
- Drafting of questionnaires
- Conducting interviews

The scope of work and timetable for completion of tasks needs to be negotiated by library staff and formalized in a written contract between the library and the consultant (see Appendix C for a sample contract agreement).

The research methods

There are at least three major research methods — collecting secondary data, collecting primary data by observation, and collecting primary data by survey — that can be used for a needs assessment study. The decision on which to select is based on what the library needs to know, the amount of time needed to complete the assessment, and the resources and expertise available. Facts and figures on the needs of at-risk youth can be gathered from content analysis of existing documents and statistics (secondary data). The credibility of the needs assessment can be greatly strengthened by gathering primary data from direct observation and/or surveys and interviews with youth and youth service providers.

Ideally, library staff should *use more than one method of data collection.* This allows statistical data to be compared and contrasted with the opinions of knowledgeable people in the community. It also subjects staff and community views to a rigorous and objective standard describing trends and the current conditions of youth. The proper mix of data collection methods should be determined in part by the availability of data in existing reports on youth issues and on the views of the study team on how much outside opinion is needed. The kinds of data collected should also be adequate to answer all the questions raised about at-risk youth and library services for teens in the community.

■ Secondary data collection

For the needs assessment, the library will want basic demographic information about youth (age, ethnicity, gender, etc.) and descriptions of existing youth resources and their use (e.g., number of teen recreation programs, teen utilization rates at health clinics, etc.). Questions should also be asked to determine the incidence of at-risk behaviors among youth. They might include the following:

- What is the drop-out rate in the school district?
- What percentage of teens are living in out-of-home placements in your county?
- How many homeless or runaway youth are in your community?
- How many juveniles were arrested in your city compared to previous years?
- What is the teen pregnancy and sexually-transmitted disease (STD) rate in your county?

• How many teens are employed full- or part-time?

Each of these questions can be answered with data from existing public records. To be most useful, the needs assessment should also:

- Gather data from previous years to highlight any trends (previous three years at minimum)
- Find comparable statistics from federal and statewide sources
- Restrict study to one geographic area (neighborhood, city, county)

Public sources of secondary data are readily accessible to most librarians. Some examples are listed in Figure 2.

Figure 2. Needs Assessment Data Sources

SOURCE	EXAMPLES OF AVAILABLE DATA
census data	age, gender, language, and ethnic distribution by county
vital statistics	teen mortality and morbidity statistics
departmental data (health, social services, probation, police, recreation, etc.)	foster care rates, incidence teen suicides, pregnancy, STDs, juvenile arrests
school district	test scores by school, school failure rates
other (Bureau of Labor Statistics, City Planning, State Legislature and Mayor's Offices, etc.)	teen labor rates, utilization rates of teen services

There are, of course, many other possible resources for collecting secondary data, including journals and newspaper articles, university-based studies, and data from youth advocacy organizations, local United Ways, Chambers of Commerce, service organizations, churches, and hospitals.

The major reason for accessing secondary data is to make use of what is already available and to build on previous efforts at data collection. It will be helpful to limit what you collect to the data needed to answer the research questions raised in the library's needs assessment study. This will avoid the "drowning in data" syndrome. Advice from the needs assessment team should help to narrow the focus of inquiry.

■ Primary data: observation

Librarians have few opportunities during their work day to observe teens in settings outside of the library. For the purposes of a needs assessment, structured observations of youth in community settings will enrich your study. Arrange visits or tours to schools or key youth-serving agencies in the targeted geographic area, such as adolescent health and mental health clinics, substance abuse programs, a foster group home, juvenile hall, or a neighborhood recreation center. Or drop in unannounced to observe a setting where youth congregate, such as an after-school recreation program, a video arcade, or a public housing project.

In both cases, prepare for the visit by finding out about the setting from brochures or telephone interviews. Consider going with a partner or group. Take notes on what you see. Compare your observations with others in the group. Such qualitative information can help your study team interpret the quantitative data it will be collecting.

■ Primary data: surveys

The major purpose of a survey is to collect information about the opinions, attitudes and beliefs of a representative group of individuals about a particular issue. The most common methods of collecting survey data are through questionnaires and interviews. They are relatively inexpensive and objective ways to collect good information from a large number of people.

There are four basic decisions to be made to develop a useful survey.

First, what information do you wish to collect in the survey? What exactly do you want to know that will be useful to you in assessing needs and developing programs (e.g., opinions, attitudes, knowledge, background information on respondents, etc.)?

Second, how will you administer and distribute the survey (individually or in focus groups, by telephone or conducting face-to-face interviews, by use of a written self-administered questionnaire)? Also, who will do it (e.g., staff, volunteers, consultants, etc.)?

Third, how many and whom (e.g., librarians, library patrons, youth, community leaders, parents) do you wish to interview or survey? Will you interview every patron or every teacher at the local high school, or select a random sample?

Finally, how will you evaluate and analyze the information once it is collected? Will you use closed or open-ended questions? Will you use computer-assisted tabulation of results?

■ What information will you collect?

The questions you ask in a community survey should ascertain the attitudes and opinions of your respondents, not just the facts and figures you can get from existing reports. Questionnaire/interview items should be tailored to the groups being surveyed, be free of technical jargon, and should again stick to the research questions posed by the needs assessment study team.

The questions should be written with the respondent in mind and can vary considerably depending on whether the respondent is a youth, a participant in a specific program, an agency manager or staff member, a community leader, or a parent. In all cases, the questions should be adapted to the knowledge level of the respondent and should be pre-tested prior to any formal interviews or mailed survey.

"When we started our needs assessment process, I thought: How can we have a focus group?
I don't know who to invite, and anyhow, I haven't got time to do this.
I can't deal with the people that walk in our doors, let alone deal with these agencies. I wish they were coming to me.
But I called them anyway, and now they *are* coming to me. Then, they weren't."

— *branch manager from Contra Costa County Library*

The major categories of questions might cover these topics:

- The background of the respondent (title, school attended, years in school or at agency, professional training, age, ethnicity, etc.)
- A description of services the agency offers (major programs, staffing, funding, and utilization rates) and how it fits into the network of youth services
- The opinions of the respondent on the problems and needs of youth in their agency and the broader community (request a rank ordering, if possible)
- The knowledge level and attitude of the respondent towards the public library (current library services for youth, new ways the library can help youth, etc.)

■ How will you administer the survey?

By far, the best way to gather opinions is to conduct in-depth interviews with a large number of respondents. Given time constraints of most library staff, the self-administered questionnaire is the more common method. In many communities, translators or bilingual interviewers are needed. Written questionnaires, however, must be translated and carefully reviewed by bilingual staff before use.

The written questionnaire, whether mailed or personally administered, has the advantage of being uniform and simple to conduct (see Appendix D for samples of questionnaires). It is inexpensive to duplicate and does not require extensive staff time. The major disadvantage is the return rate, which is frequently low. It also requires a certain level of literacy and motivation among respondents.

When preparing a questionnaire, be sure to:

☐ Write a cover letter which clearly explains the purpose of the study and invites participation.

☐ Keep the questionnaire brief, the questions concise and easy to fill out.

☐ Avoid the use of jargon, complex or double-negative questions.

☐ Make it easy to return the questionnaire (in a box on a desk, in a stamped, self-addressed envelope, etc.). Consider offering an incentive for responding (mailing the report if requested, holding a prize drawing of returned surveys, etc.).

Youth and/or service provider conferences or meetings can provide an excellent opportunity to distribute questionnaires. Schools are also an excellent source of youth and/or teacher input. A door-to-door canvassing effort can be tremendously useful if it is carefully prepared and targeted. But without a paid staff or considerable volunteer support, it is often too time-consuming to organize.

The individual or group interview is far more time-consuming but allows for a more flexible interchange between the interviewer and respondent. Training for interviewers is essential and the ques-

How-to Checklist: Preparing a Questionnaire

tions must be asked in a consistent fashion. Unstructured questions are often clustered around themes and open-ended to allow a respondent to talk more freely about selected youth issues. An unstructured interview is especially effective in the group context. When conducting an interview:

How-to Checklist: Interviewing

☐ Make an appointment and allow for sufficient time to conduct the interview.

☐ Keep it time-limited (twenty to thirty minutes).

☐ Avoid phone interviews.

☐ Keep respondents on track with the use of "probes" that help focus each answer.

Sample interview questions are shown in Appendix E.

The focus group is an increasingly popular and efficient method of interviewing. Its purpose is to explore the opinions of a group of individuals about a particular issue. The focus group consists of a free-flowing, semi-structured interview with six to twelve individuals, often conducted by a neutral facilitator/recorder team. In conducting a focus group, it is important to:

How-to Checklist: Holding a Focus Group

☐ Ask open-ended questions, moving from the general to the specific. For example,
   "What are the major problems youth face today?"
   "What are some ways public libraries can be more useful to teens in finding summer jobs?"

☐ Use bilingual focus group leaders as needed.

☐ Brainstorm before seeking consensus, so that participants feel their experiences and opinions are valued.

Participants can be a cross-section of the community or represent a specific subgroup. Focus groups can be especially effective with youth respondents. In analyzing the group interview results, some clusters of opinion or themes will generally emerge that will help guide and inform the needs assessment process. See Appendix F for sample focus group questions.

■ Who needs to be surveyed?

Ideally, the library would survey all youth and youth-service providers in the community. Since this is generally not practical, a representative sample of agency and youth respondents should be selected.

The sample selected should include a variety of youth or youth-service providers who are representative of a broad range of income and ethnic groups (see Appendix G for a sample interview list). For example, a "sampling list" of agencies can usually be obtained from a local public agency or the United Way office. If a small number of agencies is being selected, each one should represent a specific program area or target group. If a large number is being selected, a random sample (every fourth agency on the list) or a "stratified" random sample (every fourth agency from all the health agencies, every other agency serving homeless youth, and so on) should be used.

Other youth planning and advocacy organizations (such as United Way, local child advocacy groups, youth councils and coalitions) and relevant civic organizations (such as the Chamber of Commerce, ethnic clubs and church groups) should also be surveyed.

Analyzing the data

Data analysis should be addressed early in the needs assessment process. An analysis plan, developed at the outset, will save valuable time once the data are in. This is especially true for questionnaires and interviews which require each respondent's answers to be aggregated with many other answers.

Much of the secondary data mentioned earlier will not require extensive analysis. It will need to be interpreted and assessed in terms of how it will inform library services development. For example, if school drop-out rates are going up, this trend can be easily displayed, as shown in Figure 3.

Figure 3. Needs Assessment Table Sample

School Drop-Out Rate (1971-1991)*					
1971	1981	1989	1990	1991	%change (1981-91)
9.2%	9.0%	13.4%	17.8	22.5%	150%
*refers to the percent of 10th, 11th, and 12th graders who leave school before graduating					

This kind of evidence (that school drop-out rates have increased in your school district 150% over a ten year period) might become one of the primary justifications for starting a tutoring resource center for teens in a library in a targeted high-risk neighborhood.

Interview or questionnaire items on survey forms are either open-ended or closed. While the former will allow respondents the most flexibility in developing an answer, it leaves the researcher with the job of clustering a whole laundry list of overlapping categories of answers.

An example of an open-ended item might be:
Please describe the most serious problems facing youth today in this neighborhood.

A closed-ended item, on the other hand, offers pre-coded categories for answering and asks the respondent to pick one or more. There should always be an "other" category. For example:
What are the three most needed services for youth in this neighborhood?

(Check three)
☐ recreation (01)   ☐ tutoring (02)   ☐ health (03)
☐ gang prevention (04) ......etc.
☐ other (_____)

The research team must decide whether the data should be hand-tabulated or computer analyzed. Basic descriptive statistics (averages, percentages, etc.) are usually adequate to analyze needs assessment data and can often be computed with a hand calculator. If more sophisticated data analysis is called for, a research consultant should be retained to pre-code the questionnaire, enter the data, and help interpret the findings.

The final report

A written report should be drafted by the YAR team (see sample outline in Figure 4). Major findings should be highlighted and open for discussion before any priority-setting begins. Moving from the identification of needs and gaps in services to making policy and program recommendations is a critical step; it requires a special meeting at which some consensus on these key issues can be reached. The methods for conducting such a meeting are discussed in Chapter III, "Establishing an Advisory Committee." Release of the final report can be made into a public event which might attract possible press coverage (see Chapter IX, "Public Relations and Publicity").

Figure 4. Needs Assessment Report Outline

I. Executive Summary
II. Introduction
    A. Purpose of project — YA Services and YAR
    B. Sites for study
    C. Guidelines/parameters of project
III. Design
    A. Provider survey
    B. Demographics/social indicators
    C. Interviews/focus groups
    D. Other reports/data sources
IV. Description of Community Context for Youth
    A. Demographics — population, neighborhood, ethnicity, etc.
    B. Schools
    C. Major organizations/agencies — network of services
V. Key Indicators of Status of Youth — Current Trends
    A. Youth employment
    B. Health/mental health
    C. Substance abuse
    D. Child welfare
    E. Juvenile justice
    F. School performance
VI. Major Problems/Unmet Needs (from provider survey and interviews)
    A. Problems (as perceived by youth and adults)
    B. Unmet needs — prioritized
VII. YA Services Ideas/Proposals
    A. Collaborative projects
    B. New or expanded programs
    C. Outreach strategies
    D. Neighborhood branch/population-focused services
VIII. Implementation Plan/Recommendations
    A. Timetable
    B. Key participants

The YAR Project and Needs Assessment

In order to ensure some consistency across all nine BALIS member library systems, the YAR Project director developed a prototype research design for all nine needs assessments. In addition, the YAR Project developed multiple research strategies to collect data for local YAR planning teams to use in their service plan development. In order to maximize the variety of sources of information, the YAR Project director mailed questionnaires to over four hundred youth service providers in all nine Bay Area communities to assess youth needs and solicit input on how libraries can improve their work with youth at risk.

YAR teams assembled in each site helped the library and a research consultant to design and conduct the local needs assessment. During a three to four month process, the YAR teams and consultant tailored the research design to the needs and priorities of each community. In some sites, this meant an emphasis on focus groups and face-to-face interviews. In others, there was a greater reliance on secondary data and the mailed provider questionnaire (especially if the response rate was high). The data collection methods used in Alameda County, for example, included:

- *Focus groups with youth*
- *Telephone and face-to-face interviews with key informants*
- *Student surveys conducted in several local schools*
- *A random survey conducted at a local youth conference*
- *Secondary data collected from public records and reports*

Each YAR team also advised on the most effective programs the library could develop based on the information collected in the needs assessment. In some cases, a priority need was not viewed as the one most suited for an effective programmatic response by the public library system (for example, some libraries felt priority needs such as dealing with gangs or teen suicide were beyond their current abilities). Whenever possible, however, YAR pilot projects tried to address at least one of the priority needs in each site. The prototype research design used for needs assessments is outlined in Appendix H.

Assessing the Needs of Youth at Risk

Background

You have been asked to coordinate creation of a needs assessment strategy as a preface to developing new library services for at-risk youth in your community. You must convene a local needs assessment planning team to advise your library system on youth needs. You must also gather data about the status of teenagers in your community. Select a time and budget that fits conditions at your library.

Task

■ **Identify an appropriate strategy to involve the community in a needs assessment.**

1. Whom should you include on the local Youth at Risk Planning Team? List ten categories of members.

2. Whom should you contact in the community to begin the needs assessment process? List ten key contacts.

■ **Collect the most relevant information on teens and their families from existing secondary data.**

1. What do you need to know about the demographic characteristics of your youth population? (e.g., age distribution, gender, etc.)

2. List the five most useful demographic characteristics you would need to collect. Where would you find them?

■ **Develop a manageable and appropriate strategy for assessing the opinions of key community leaders, youth-service providers, parents, and youth.**

1. Who are the key informants/respondents who should be surveyed or interviewed about youth needs in your community?

2. List five possible groups of respondents and indicate whether you would send them a questionnaire or ask them to participate in a focus group.

■ **Develop a list of key variables or indicators (often in the form of questionnaire items) that you want to measure in your data collection efforts.**

1. What items should be included in a questionnaire to youth-service providers in your community?

2. Draft five possible items (and categories for answering closed-ended questions) you might include in a questionnaire.

3. What open-ended questions might you ask in a group interview (focus group)?

4. List three key questions or themes to include in the focus group.

■ **Develop a realistic workplan for completing key tasks in the needs assessment.**

CHAPTER II. # Involving the Community in Services to Youth at Risk

Community involvement is critical to the delivery of effective young adult library services to at-risk youth. Library services need to be made more accessible to teens, especially to those not currently using libraries. To facilitate this process, youth-service providers (agency staff and secondary school teachers) and teens themselves need to be better informed about the range and availability of library services to youth. Librarians also need to be more knowledgeable about the network of youth services in their community. Collaborative projects which link libraries and youth services systems are an important strategy for developing innovative community involvement programs.

Despite the staff time that must be devoted to involving the community, the benefits usually far outweigh the costs. By reaching out to community organizations and youth, librarians will learn about current teen concerns in their own areas and gain valuable information on other programs being offered or planned. Promoting community involvement will increase visibility for public library services as well as provide a unique opportunity to publicize YA programs and receive timely and constructive feedback. The development of off-site library services can also make it possible to reach unserved (e.g., institutionalized) and/or underserved teens.

WHY involve the community in services to youth at risk

- To make contacts with youth service providers and at-risk youth regarding the range of library resources available to teens
- To inform librarians working with young adults about the school and community context in which youth live
- To recognize and reduce formidable physical and psychological barriers to increased use of library services by at-risk youth

WHAT a librarian should do to involve the community

Networking

- Find out how things get done for and with youth in your community.
- Get to know teens in the community who will share their knowledge of library services.
- Foster formal library participation on youth coordinating councils, agency boards, and child advocacy groups in the community.
- Invite youth and youth-serving agencies to be involved in the work of the library through joint projects, advisory councils, or special task forces.

Collaborative projects — your place or mine?

- Locate library services in user-friendly community settings, like schools, shopping malls, recreation centers, and video arcades to increase their visibility and reduce psychological as well as physical barriers between young people and library services.
- Take library services to off-site locations that reach unserved (e.g., institutionalized) or underserved teens.
- Invite youth service agencies to provide counseling, tutoring, support groups, and speaker forums in the library as scheduling and space allows, to bring at-risk youth into the library setting.

HOW to involve the community in services to youth at risk

There are a wide range of possible strategies to involve the community in programs for youth at risk, limited only by the imagination, energy and resources of library staff. Discuss your ideas with other youth-serving professionals in the community and then test them out to see which ones are most effective, given the needs of the community and the strengths and resources of library staff.

Network

Public libraries have always been a key component in the network of youth services which includes public and private non-profit agencies as well as informal support systems, such as churches, clubs, business and community associations. To maximize the library's role within this network of youth services, librarians need to become more pro-active by forming partnerships with other youth-service providers.

The library should learn first whether any sort of network or forum of youth-serving agencies is already in place. If so, the library can

Figure 5. Sample young adult resource guide

Young Adult Resource Guide San Lorenzo Area

Alameda County Library

24 HOUR CRISIS LINES
AIDS Hotline...1-800-FOR-AIDS
Alameda County Child Protective Services 483-9300
Alameda County Health Care Services.........................677-7800
Alameda County Psychiatric Emergency......................534-8055
Bay Area Women Against Rape 845-RAPE
California Youth Crisis Line..................................834-5200
Poison Control Center..476-6600
Suicide Prevention..889-1333

ALCOHOL & DRUGS
Al-Anon/Alateen 276-2270
Alcoholics Anonymous 886-2123
Narcotics Anonymous 843-3701
Second Chance..886-8696
Thunder Road 653-5040

CHILD CARE REFERRAL
4 C's 582-2189
Davis Street Center...635-8500

COUNSELING
Birthright ("Pro-Life").......................................839-9203
Birthways..464-3095
Crisis Pregnancy Center ("Pro-Life")..........................487-4357
Eden Children's Center 667-7540
Family Service of the East Bay...............................887-1843
Girl's Inc., Hayward...887-0113
Girl's Inc., San Leandro.....................................357-5515
Hayward Youth & Family Service 784-7048
La Familia Counseling Service................................881-5921
Pathways Counseling Center..................................357-5515
Project Eden...887-0566
San Leandro Community Counseling............................638-6603
Southern Alameda County YWCA..............................785-2736

GAY & LESBIAN YOUTH
Pacific Center for Human Growth..............................841-6224

HEALTH
AIDS Project of the East Bay.................................834-8181
Clinic for Adults and Children...............................483-4550
Hayward Community Health Center 667-5300
Miranda Clinic 786-6517
Native American Clinic 261-8943
Planned Parenthood...733-1814
Tiburcio Vasquez Clinic 783-5360
Tri-City Clinic 797-1188

more on back . . .

JOB TRAINING
East Bay Conservation Corps..................................891-3900
Eden Area Jobs for Youth....................................537-JOBS
Eden Area ROP...293-2913
Vallecitos CET 537-8400

LAW ENFORCEMENT
Alameda County Sheriff's Department.........................667-7721
Hayward Police Department..................................293-7000
San Leandro Police Department...............................577-3241

LIBRARIES
Bookmobile 745-1477
Castro Valley Public Library.................................670-6280
Fremont Main Library.......................................745-1401
Hayward Public Library......................................293-8685
San Leandro City Library....................................577-3490
San Lorenzo Public Library...................................670-6283

SCHOOLS
Arroyo High School 276-2260
Bohannon High School......................................481-2171
Hayward Unified School District Office........................784-2600
San Leandro Unified School District Office....................667-3500
San Lorenzo High School 276-3121
San Lorenzo Unified School District Office....................276-3600

OTHER YOUTH SERVICES
4-H Youth Development......................................670-5210
Eden Area YMCA...582-9614
Eden Youth Center 887-1146
Hayward Area Recreation & Park District 881-6700
Hayward Boys & Girls Club..................................886-5511
San Leandro Boys & Girls Club...............................483-5581

PERSONAL NUMBERS

_____

_____

_____

_____

_____

_____

_____

_____

_____

And . . . if you can't find the name of the group you're looking for, or don't know the right phone number, call the library, check the phone book, or call 411 for directory assistance.

This guide was produced by the San Lorenzo Library, a branch of Alameda County Library (5/92). It was made possible through the BALIS Bay Area Youth-At-Risk Project, funded by the California State Library through a Library Services & Construction Act (LSCA) grant, with partial funding by the San Francisco Foundation.

join, attend meetings, and learn about youth issues in the community as well as communicate with network members about library projects and resources. There may be a need for information compilation for the network that the library can fill, for example, by producing a directory of youth resources (see Figure 5 for a sample young adult resource guide).

In some communities there may not be an existing forum for sharing ideas among youth-service providers. In this case, the library can — in consultation with youth service providers and interested community members — convene a forum itself. By contacting youth service workers with an invitation to a meeting and setting an appropriate agenda, the library can play an important role in the community and increase its visibility. The first meeting of a forum should include all interested parties and allow for introductions and exchange of ideas. Meetings needn't be held frequently — every other month or quarterly, for example — and may be most effective as informal structures, since participants will probably already be involved in many other more formal or mandated committees or groups.

An initial general meeting may offer youth service providers one of few opportunities they have to talk face to face. By hosting such a meeting, the library can take a leadership role and gain recognition for its own services to teens. The library can continue to convene network meetings with a minimum of effort, benefitting other agencies by providing a neutral site and gaining ongoing visibility for the resources it has to offer. With ongoing meetings, the library should make every effort to emphasize these strengths.

When networking, the library should avoid duplication or competition with programs or networks that may already be in place. It should be cognizant of developing issues in the youth community such as funding cuts or changes in relationships between different agencies. The library should also be careful not to leave other agencies with unrealistic expectations about what it can do. With these caveats in mind, networking can bring significant benefits in return for a relatively low level of effort.

Additional points to keep in mind when networking include:

☐ Find an up-to-date list or directory of youth-service providers or, if necessary, develop one yourself. An example of an existing directory is the Bay Area Information Referral System (BAIRS) in the San Francisco Bay Area.

☐ Identify the major sectors of youth services (education, health, mental health, social services, recreation, juvenile justice, substance abuse, etc.) and at least one contact person. Call to find out some of the major issues in each field. If there is a local youth hotline or switchboard it can be a valuable place to start. Note: The first phone call is the hardest! Once you have started, the rest will come much easier.

"Networking sounds overwhelming at first. But just take one small step after another to involve a person or group in planning and carrying out library services, and you suddenly realize one day that you've done it.
It's a pleasure and a reward. It makes doing a good job easy."

— *librarian from Contra Costa County Library*

How-to Checklist: Networking

(continued on next page)

**How-to Checklist:
Networking**
(continued)

☐ Call the Mayor's Office, County Board of Supervisors, or United Way to find out if there is an existing coordinating council of youth-serving agencies in your community.

☐ Find out the timing for and what is on the agenda of any upcoming youth-related coordinating council or commission meetings.

☐ Make sure the library gets on mailing lists for upcoming youth-related meetings.

☐ Make a special effort to find out from the local school district about the composition of the student body as well as programs and activities in the various junior high and high schools in your service area.

☐ Make contact with local principals, teachers, counselors, school librarians, etc.

☐ Obtain studies/needs assessments and use them to help identify key problems facing youth in your community.

☐ Assess the youth service network —- where do kids go after school? (the Y, Boys and Girls Club, recreation center, arcade, street corner, etc.).

☐ If there is no appropriate forum for library participation within the youth services network, call your own meeting (for help with this, see the How-to Checklist: Holding Successful Meetings in Chapter III, "Establishing an Advisory Committee").

Collaborate

Exciting possibilities exist for libraries to collaborate with a wide range of organizations in the community to offer services to youth at risk. Collaboration not only with other youth-serving agencies but also with other types of organizations (e.g., Parks and Recreation departments, shopping malls) can bring these benefits:

- Help the library discover its own most effective role to serve youth at risk
- Increase the library's visibility in the community
- Generate more successful services for teens

Libraries may find that rigid bureaucracy has previously inhibited collaboration among youth programs. Particularly in the youth services field, fragmentation — rather than integration — of services has been well documented. Still, efforts to coordinate or collaborate are generally well received by service providers and increase the quality and accessibility of programs for teens themselves.

Some tips to aid collaboration with other agencies include:

☐ Make a list of any existing collaborative, interagency services in which your library is involved. Review the documents or evaluations which might have been developed on the success of these joint projects.

☐ Publicize the availability of meeting areas in your library to youth-service providers and offer to co-sponsor some of their events.

☐ In consultation with an array of local youth agencies and schools, develop a series of youth outreach programs with a theme (e.g., tutoring, sex education, cultural roots, jobs for teens) and contact appropriate agencies to offer your support services on a trial basis.

☐ Develop a written memo of understanding (MOU) or contract, if necessary, to formalize interagency programs, so that lines of accountability are very clear.

☐ Use the collaborative nature of your project to obtain additional funds for supporting or expanding the project. Successful collaborative projects are very popular in the foundation world and are likely to attract outside grant monies. Collaboration can help ensure that there won't be a duplication of effort by funding groups sponsoring youth at risk projects.

Don't overlook the possibility of collaborating with nearby libraries, in addition to other youth-serving agencies. Neighborhood youth aren't contained by the same jurisdictional boundaries that define libraries, and other local jurisdictions — school districts, for example — may include two or more libraries within their limits. Collaborating with other libraries offers many opportunities to share both workloads and resources. It can also offer staff training benefits, including an increase in communication about training tools.

CASE EXAMPLE

The YAR Project and Community Involvement

One of the major findings of the YAR Project needs assessments in each of the nine participating communities was that libraries had to do a much better job of reaching out not only to youth but also to youth-service providers in the communities they served. In response to this need, library staff participating in the YAR Project developed a rich array of innovative strategies to involve the community in services to youth at risk.

In some sites (e.g., San Francisco Public Library), libraries worked with other agencies to deliver library services off-site. In several sites (e.g., Alameda Free Library), libraries joined existing youth-serving coordinating councils. In others (e.g., Contra Costa County Library), it was necessary for library staff to create their own forums city-wide or by neighborhood.

San Francisco Public Library began its program of delivering library services off-site after its needs assessment recommended establishing a library program for youth incarcerated at the juvenile hall. Initial meetings with the chief probation officer were very positive and indicated a strong willingness to host a library program at San Francisco's Youth Guidance Center.

Staff from both agencies evaluated options and eventually drafted a written proposal to begin a regular library service in one of the highest security cottages for incarcerated boys ages ten to seventeen. Library staff conducted a user survey before selecting reading materials for the program.

New city funds authorized specifically for funding collaborative children and youth services were also committed to support the project after its initial YAR Project pilot stage. This collaborative outreach project may serve as a model for the development of similar library services in the community.

In Alameda, a Youth Gang Prevention Task Force had been named in 1990 to address a growing gang problem among teens in the city. Alameda Free Library staff began to attend on a regular basis. As the focus of the meetings changed, the organization — now called the Alameda Youth Activities Network — also broadened its focus. Library staff became an integral part of the network by providing the other members access to information about current resources and summer activities.

More important for the YAR Project, Alameda library staff were able to use the monthly meeting forums to publicize and obtain support for the library's YAR pilot project and on-going development of services for teens. The library has become an important and active participant in the local network of services to youth.

At Contra Costa County Library's San Pablo Branch, quarterly forums for youth-serving agencies grew out of focus groups held during the library's youth needs assessment. Input provided through the needs assessment process showed that having a

"It's pretty cool, man. You know, not a whole lot of people give a shit about us in here or even think we can read, but I can and I know most everybody in here can too. And we don't have anything but time on our hands, so reading is all we can do a lot of the time. I'm just gonna work to try and improve myself so I don't have to come back here."

— incarcerated teen when asked what he thought of library visits to the San Francisco Youth Guidance Center

32

common meeting ground was a high priority for youth service providers. The idea of quarterly forums was born. In conjunction with nearby Richmond Public Library, the San Pablo Branch provides the meeting place, offers refreshments and mails agendas; other participants do the rest. For that relatively low level of effort, the library gains visibility and is able to purchase materials for youth service providers based on their explicitly stated needs.

"At first, when I set out to organize the focus groups, I didn't think we had the resources to track these people down, that it would be a full time job," said the San Pablo branch manager. "Of course I went ahead and did it anyway and every single agency could refer me to two others and the network grew and grew. What was so surprising wasn't that they said, 'Oh, yeah, we all know each other anyway and the library is a johnny-come-lately.' I found out that they didn't know each other, that they were anxious to get to know each other, and they certainly had no place where they could go sit down and meet each other face to face to air issues. They responded with things like: 'Wow, you're a librarian — you're calling me? I would love to help you out. Wow, I didn't even know there was a library there. You can be such a big help to us in our work.' It was an entirely positive response."

Involving the Community

Background

Library use by teens is minimal at your library except for term paper and homework help sought by motivated students, especially during finals week. Little is known about your services and resources for teens by youth-serving agencies or at-risk youth in the community. You have been asked to increase youth awareness of library services and build a programmatic relationship with other community agencies serving youth.

Tasks

■ **Develop a strategy for getting your public library involved in the network of youth services in your community.**

1. What youth-related committees, coordinating councils or boards meet on a regular basis in your community? (Identify three)

2. Identify at least eight service delivery systems for children and youth in your community (e.g., schools, juvenile justice, etc.) and whom you might contact to find out more about each one.

■ **Develop partnerships with youth-serving public, private or non-profit organizations in your community. Briefly describe a collaborative project that could be developed in partnership with another agency. Include a description of the youth population to be served, the goal of the joint project, and the benefits to the youth served.**

CHAPTER III.

Establishing a Youth-Related Advisory Committee

Librarians need to develop an organizational structure that fosters two-way communication between library staff and the youth they serve. An advisory committee of youth service providers and/or youth themselves can provide such a vehicle. It must be well organized, representative of the community being served, and offer benefits to both the library and the appointed members.

WHY develop an advisory committee

- To gather input from various segments of the community in order to build consensus and develop responsive library service
- To heighten the profile of the public library's role in the community
- To enhance program legitimacy in the community being served and resolve program issues which may arise
- To broaden and improve community relations

WHAT a librarian should do to develop an advisory committee

Develop a clear mission statement and membership criteria
- Draft a clear written mandate for the committee, describing the purpose of the committee and its anticipated length of duty.
- Determine the terms of membership and the representation on the committee including a strong youth presence.

Plan meeting logistics
- Determine the most convenient time and location for the meetings.
- Develop a mailing list and a way to keep committee members informed.

Manage meetings
- Determine what should be included in an agenda.
- Review the techniques of running a productive meeting.

HOW to create and sustain an advisory committee

There are at least three major factors to consider when setting up an advisory committee:
- its purpose and membership
- meeting logistics
- how to run a good meeting

Purpose and membership

An advisory committee should have a clear purpose for its existence. Some committees are legally mandated, with pre-determined goals, membership and process. Most are not mandated, and thus require a clear statement of their purpose and who should serve on the committee. Generally, an advisory committee can give advice to help shape teen programs and can assist with outreach and publicity. Both the limits and the opportunities of the committee's mandate need to be articulated to potential members.

Membership should reflect the community as much as possible in an effort to include the necessary expertise and range of opinions in the group. Gender, ethnicity, age, and other factors should be considered in selecting participants. Names of prospective members should be compiled from lists of active community leaders and youth provided by local schools and other youth organizations. These can be supplemented with names developed by word of mouth, reputation, and perceived interest level. Usually, an advisory group consists of both library users and non-users.

When creating an advisory committee, remember to:

How-to Checklist: Creating an Advisory Committee

☐ Determine the mission of the committee and set specific goal(s) for each meeting.

☐ Explore staffing support for needed resources (mailings, meeting site, etc.).

☐ Select a representative and active membership.

☐ Appoint or elect a chair and subcommittees.

☐ Compile current addresses and phone lists of members.

Meeting logistics

Meeting arrangements must be made with the committee's needs in mind. If youth are involved, meetings will have to take place after school or on the weekends and often on a school site. Evening meetings are usually easier for people who can't get time off from work, but it is harder to attract some youth workers who can take work time to serve on job-related committees. Late afternoon, early morning, or lunchtime meetings are often preferable times to meet.

Libraries often have an available meeting room along with access to scheduling of the facility. Meetings should also be considered in off-site locations to accommodate all members.

To help ensure successful meetings:

How-to Checklist: Holding Successful Meetings

☐ Schedule meetings at a convenient time and location for all members (especially youth).

☐ Start planning meetings well in advance (three to four weeks, if possible).

☐ Send out the agenda and background materials before each meeting.

☐ Make reminder phone calls the day before the meeting.

☐ Serve light refreshments.

☐ Put up signs pointing out the meeting location at the entrance and have a sign-in list at the door.

☐ Make name tags for participants before each meeting. Make sure names are large enough to be read.

☐ Make introductions at the beginning of every meeting.

☐ Select a neutral chairperson who will foster participation, help the group reach consensus, and keep the meetings focused and on schedule.

☐ Use a research consultant to present findings clearly and simply to group members (optional).

☐ Summarize consensus points and tasks for follow-up at the conclusion of each meeting.

☐ Use a flipchart or chalkboard to record key issues raised.

☐ Take abbreviated minutes or ask for a volunteer to take minutes.

☐ Develop a current mailing list. Include phone and fax numbers.

☐ Mail agendas, minutes, meeting announcements, etc. to all members.

Managing meetings

Building an agenda and running a productive and time-limited meeting can help a committee accomplish its task. A sample agenda is shown in Figure 6. Agenda items should be included after consultation with the chair and key members of the committee. Items can also be added at the beginning of each meeting. Time limits should be attached to each item if possible to allow the committee to finish its business.

Most meetings need not be run using *Robert's Rules of Order,* but the chairperson should be able to move through the agenda. The role for the chairperson is key to keeping a meeting on track and making sure all opinions have been voiced (especially youth members) before decisions are made. It is helpful to encourage each person attending a meeting to express his/her opinion on important issues. This will allow both formal and informal leadership to emerge and keep all members coming back.

Minutes need not be exhaustive but should include attendance and actions taken by the committee. They should be mailed out to all members with meeting announcements and agendas prior to a subsequent meeting. A date for a next meeting (and follow-up meetings too, if possible) should always be determined before adjournment.

"You have to be prepared to glue the telephone to your ear. That's how it's done, over the phone, catching somebody in the ten minutes between clients or in between other meetings."

— librarian working on the BALIS YAR Project

Figure 6. Sample Meeting Agenda

YAR STEERING COMMITTEE MEETING AGENDA

4:00 - 4:15	Welcome and Introductions—*Gary* -time to glance through needs assessment draft report
4:15 - 4:30	Review of Methods Used to Collect Needs Assessment Data—*Stan & Robin* -interviews -focus groups -mailed questionnaire
4:30 - 4:45	Presentation of Draft Report—*Robin* -basic demographics -major identified needs -YA services recommendations
4:45 - 4:55	Break—*All*
4:55 - 5:45	Discussion—*Caryn & Judy* -review & critique report -consensus on priorities -what is feasible -additional information needed
5:45 - 6:00	Future Role of YAR Steering Committee—*Gary* -ongoing advisory role -review pilot project in second year -timeline for remainder of needs assessment

Figure 7. Bay Area YAR Project Organizational Structure

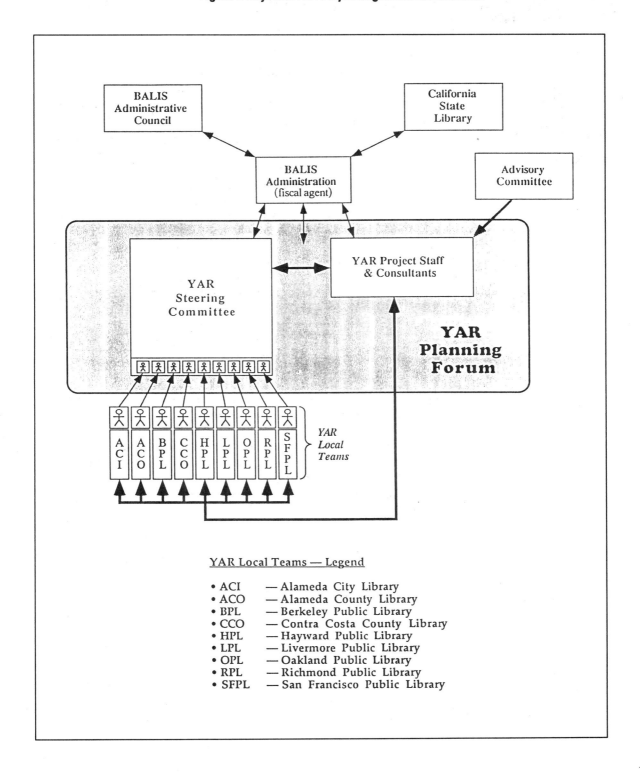

YAR Local Teams — Legend

- ACI — Alameda City Library
- ACO — Alameda County Library
- BPL — Berkeley Public Library
- CCO — Contra Costa County Library
- HPL — Hayward Public Library
- LPL — Livermore Public Library
- OPL — Oakland Public Library
- RPL — Richmond Public Library
- SFPL — San Francisco Public Library

Advisory Committees for the YAR Project

The YAR Project worked extensively with its existing oversight and advisory committee network (shown in the Bay Area YAR Project organizational structure in Figure 7). The BALIS Administrative Council, composed of all nine library directors, gave its initial support for the original LSCA grant proposal and remained a key supporter of the project. Project staff also worked closely with the YAR Steering Committee, which included representatives from each of the nine library systems; the BALIS Public Information Committee, which included community relations personnel from each system; and the System Advisory Board, which included appointed citizen representatives from each library system in BALIS.

The YAR Project also created a blue-ribbon Advisory Committee which was kept informed of the project's progress, but never held a formal meeting. It gave name recognition to the project in each of the nine communities. Each member was listed on project letterhead. Local YAR planning teams were created in each of the nine participating communities to assist in the needs assessment process. In some of those sites, committees continued to meet to help monitor YAR pilot projects.

In the case of Alameda County Library, an active YAR planning team was engaged in the needs assessment process and carried on during the pilot project implementation in an advisory capacity. More important, the YA librarian on the staff of Alameda County's San Lorenzo Branch convened a youth advisory committee which continued to meet regularly to help plan further teen programs, develop brochures, work with the media, and consult on YA services generally.

Creating and Chairing an Advisory Committee

Background

You have been asked to create and convene a young adult community advisory committee which will help guide the development of improved library services to teens in your community.

Tasks

■ Develop a set of goals for the advisory committee with a timetable and tentative workplan. Draft the first paragraph of a letter to prospective members of the advisory committee in which you clearly state the mission of the group as well as the time commitment that is being asked of participants.

■ List six tentative topics for a series of meetings over the next three months. Include a detailed agenda for the first meeting.

■ Develop a membership that is representative of the community you are trying to serve. List ten prospective members (names or affiliations), both adults and youth, who should be invited to the first meeting.

■ Determine when and where the advisory committee meeting should be held. Select the most convenient time and place for the committee to meet and justify your decision in terms of the impact on attendance.

CHAPTER IV.   **Plan Development**

A YAR service plan should link the unmet needs of youth in your community with the library's mission and roles. It should describe goals, objectives and specific activities as well as a means of evaluating the effects of current and new programs and services. Frequently, good ideas fail to get implemented because a planning phase is not built in to the project.

WHY develop a planning process for YAR

- To develop a step-by-step process which establishes a set of clear goals and objectives
- To assess available resources and produce a realistic timetable and budget that makes it possible to reach selected goals

WHAT is involved in developing a YAR service plan

Effective planning takes place in two phases. The first can be called the pre-planning phase and primarily focuses on the people and systems needed to be involved in the planning process. The second is the development of the actual written planning document, with clear goals and objectives and steps for full and effective implementation.

The pre-planning phase should involve an assessment of the readiness of library administration and library staff to develop a plan for service. Library staff must be able to coordinate the planning process with other management activities, "look around" for information already available on the library and the population to be served, and develop a set of clear roles and a mission before moving forward with the development of actual goals and objectives (see Public Library Development Project, *Planning and Role Setting for Public Libraries*, 1987). Without broad library staff and community involvement and support, the planning process is unlikely to succeed.

The second phase involves the development of a written YAR service plan and should include the following components:

- An executive summary
- Background of your community, including basic demographic information
- A mission statement for YAR services; a description of how the YAR plan relates to the library's overall mission and goals
- A needs statement describing conditions of youth in your community: statistics, identified problems and needs, and existing services
- Goals for the library's existing or new YAR services or programs
- Measurable objectives which define the steps, responsible parties and a timeline for achieving the goals
- Budget for resources needed to accomplish the goals and objectives, including staff, library materials, operating expenses and equipment
- A means for evaluating the effectiveness of the plan and reporting results to library administrators and the public
- A strategy for continuing YAR services and programs after they have been shown to be effective

HOW to write a YAR service plan

The YAR service plan should be prepared as a draft for discussion among key participants before it is finalized. Each plan component is outlined below (adapted from materials prepared by Jayne Becker, YAR Project consultant).

Executive summary

The executive summary is an overview of the key elements of your YAR plan. It should convey all the essential points without need for further explanation. Your summary should include the following:

- The name of your agency
- Whom you will serve; your target population's need
- What services or programs you propose; how they will fill the need
- Your library's mission; how the new programs or services advance the mission
- Conditions which make your library well qualified to provide the services or programs
- Agencies or groups with whom your library will collaborate
- The budget and timeline for the YAR plan period
- Methods for evaluating and continuing the new services or programs, as well as continuing the needs assessment process

Needs statement

To write this section, draw upon your needs assessment report. Your needs statement should answer the following questions:

- Who are the people about whom you are concerned?
- What problem or need will you address? This should be stated in terms of the client population's needs, but should be a need upon which the library could reasonably be expected to have an impact.
- How is this need documented? This could be through the library's own experience, testimony of the target group, authoritative statistics, etc.
- What services do the library and/or other community agencies currently provide to serve this need for the target population? What resources does the library currently have?

Mission

Draw upon the library's existing documents for this section. Include a statement of your library's overall mission or purpose, and its primary/secondary roles. Include any language from the library's plan of service about the philosophy of service, priorities, and/or current emphasis of youth services.

Your YAR mission proposal should be briefly stated, and the relationship of your proposal to your library's overall mission and primary/secondary roles made clear. Address what the library's service plan says about this population and its needs, and the library's intent to provide services. Outline how the library will work in collaboration with other agency(ies) to provide new programs and services.

Program goals

Goals are long-range, broad statements of what will be done to achieve the mission. They are action-oriented and often describe what will be different by the end of the planning period.

State no more than four to six goals for the YAR plan. The program goals should logically flow from the convergence of target population needs and the library's mission. Having come this far, the reader should clearly recognize the relationship of your goals to the unmet needs of your targeted population. Some examples follow:

- To improve services to recent Hispanic immigrant youth
- To offer homework support to junior high school students

Objectives

Objectives are specific measurable steps for achieving a goal. Objectives identify a responsible party to take specific action within a defined time period. The objectives also provide a timeline for the project. You may include how you will publicize the new programs or services. Some examples follow:

- By _____ 199___ , the young adult librarian will create a resource center and study area for junior high school students.
- Quarterly, the library director will contract with a trainer to offer workshops in study skills and practical tips for junior high school students.

Evaluation

The plan's section on evaluation should answer the following questions:

- How will you know your program or service is a success? Clearly describe what elements of the project will be evaluated and the criteria by which you will judge the effects of your efforts. The evaluation criteria should be closely related to the goals.
- What measures will be used to determine whether those criteria have been met? Try to design some evaluation measures that will show how well the need has been met within the target population. Output measures, such as reduced school dropout rates or increased knowledge about library resources, can be used to assess the impact of a specific project. Subjective evaluation measures of changes in attitudes or behaviors might include pre- and post-testing, surveys or interviews of target populations and collaborating agencies.

In addition, traditional quantifiable measures of changes in library use patterns might include positive trends in registration per capita, circulation per capita, turnover rate, program attendance, library attendance, in-library use rates, reference transactions, or materials added. Consider questions such as the following:

- How, when, and how often will this information be gathered? By whom?
- How will this evaluation be reported? To whom?
- How will this evaluation be used to modify the program or service during the initial period? After?

Budget

The plan should present a budget covering the following categories:

- *Salaries and benefits*. Provide line items for the salary of each project staff person who is a regular employee. Provide a figure for the total benefits for all staff. Do not include persons on contract.
- *Library materials*. Give the total amount for books, periodicals, tapes and videos to be purchased for use by the client group.

- *Operations.* Provide a line item for each component of operating expenses, e.g. office and library supplies, postage, telephone, contract and maintenance expense, local travel, printing and duplicating, public relations, training fees and expenses, small equipment, persons on contract.
- *Equipment.* Give an amount for major equipment to be purchased exclusively for the use of the project.

Budget narrative

This section supplements the budget, providing additional detail for proposed expenditures. Here one should also describe any other funds from the library or collaborating agencies that will be used to support the new programs/services. In addition, identify any in-kind services and support that will be provided. Specific considerations for each budget category are given below.

- *Salaries and benefits.* Indicate the job titles of each staff person needed to operate the project. Describe what each person will do and what percentage of their time will be required. Indicate the lines of authority within the project and between the project and the library.
- *Library materials.* Describe what is to be purchased and how it will be used.
- *Operations.* Provide any explanations you believe may be necessary about proposed operating expenses, particularly public relations, training fees and expenses, small equipment, contract personnel, and printing.
- *Equipment.* Describe each equipment purchase and how it will be used.

Next steps and continuation

This section should describe the immediate next steps in having a plan approved, as well as the steps you will take to make sure that the library can build on the foundation laid by the planning process. Include answers to the following questions:

- What are the steps to having a YAR plan approved? Who will be involved? Who will be responsible for each step? What is the time frame for approval?
- How will you publish the plan? How, when and to whom will you present it? How will you publicize the plan?
- How will the plan be funded? What activities will you undertake to ensure that there is support for the new programs/services to continue?
- How will you continue to serve youth at risk? How will you continue to work with youth-serving agencies in the future?
- How will the plan affect your library's YA plan of service? The library's overall plan of service?

"It's improved my son's reading level. Now he even reads to his younger brother. But that's not all. His grades have gone up, too."

— *parent commenting on Oakland Public Library tutoring program*

Plan Development in the YAR Project

After an extensive needs assessment process, each BALIS library designated a staff person to play a lead role in drafting a YAR plan for his/her library. Staff from all nine libraries participated in a three-hour training session, which was based on the information presented in this chapter and facilitated by a consultant.

The most difficult part of the planning process was the effort to match the highest priority needs identified in the needs assessment report with the most effective programmatic response (see needs and pilot projects summary chart in Figure 8). Planning staff had to balance what was most needed (for instance, drug treatment or gang prevention) with what they felt the library system, or one branch, could most effectively accomplish, given its resource limitations and staff expertise. Service plans were varied and reflected input from many different sources.

Each library drafted, circulated and discussed its YAR service plan before developing a budget for a YAR Project pilot project. Each library then approved the plan, the pilot project and the budget for submission to BALIS. The libraries began implementing the various pilot projects in the fall of 1991.

The San Francisco YAR planning process coincided with two other interrelated planning efforts underway at San Francisco Public Library — the development of a young adult services plan as well as space planning for the new main library which required input from YA and children's librarians. Some of the data collected as part of the YAR needs assessment were used to help make policy decisions affecting the other two plans. The library also set up a YAR subcommittee of its YA committee to facilitate ongoing communication between all relevant staff.

Proposals in the YAR plan included the following:
- *Community outreach in two high-risk neighborhoods*
- *Out-stationed library services at the juvenile hall*
- *Youth overdue fee amnesty*

A copy of the San Francisco YAR Service Plan Proposal (excluding budget) is included in Appendix I.

Figure 8. YAR Project Needs and Pilot Projects

LIBRARY	PRIORITY NEED	SELECTED PILOT PROJECT
Alameda County (San Lorenzo Branch)	Multicultural exchange; job training	Teen forums on key issues; distribute resource guide; "Stump the Librarian" contest
Alameda Free	Awareness of youth-related services/programs; improved school performance	Tutoring clearing house; Teen Room improvement
Berkeley	Teen employment and youth involvement in library programming	Youth Outreach Corps and media outreach (PSA)
Contra Costa County (San Pablo Branch)	Awareness of services; coordination with youth-serving agencies	Video outreach project to schools and youth-serving agencies; give out hip-pocket guide to services
Hayward	Access to neighborhood-based services and information on resources; school drop-out prevention	Youth forums and school outreach; hip-pocket resource guide; teen issues pamphlet and resource file
Livermore	Improved school performance; teen employment opportunities	Develop teen area; teen information booklet "Unhappy at Home"
Oakland (M.L. King Branch)	Improved coordination with agencies/schools; school drop-out prevention	Tutoring outreach in public housing
Richmond	School drop-out prevention; coordination with youth-serving agencies	Tutoring program support to youth-serving agencies; hip-pocket resource guide
San Francisco	Access to information by/for African-American and immigrant youth	Youth fee amnesty; develop out-stationed library services in public housing, Youth Guidance Center, etc.; cooperative projects with youth-serving organizations

Goals and Objectives in Plan Development

Background

You have been asked to write a library service plan for youth at risk in your community. You have finished a needs assessment and have identified key areas of concern for local youth. You have three months to prepare a plan for the next two years.

Tasks

■ Develop a set of goals for the service plan based on your library's mission. List three possible goals for serving youth at risk.

■ Develop measurable objectives to achieve your goals. For each goal developed above, list two objectives to help meet that goal. Be sure each objective states a specific action and a time within which it must be taken.

CHAPTER V.   # Proposal Writing

The expansion and improvement of library services for teens usually involves a change in priorities and/or a restructuring of existing services. This is especially true when there is no existing young adult services division in the library. Often the only way to document the value of a new program or approach to serving youth is to develop funding support to demonstrate its value. Therefore, proposal writing for internal or external funding can be a key strategy for developing innovative services for youth at risk.

WHY write proposals for teen library services

- To attract supplemental funding for innovative programs that may not fall within the library's traditional budget categories
- To demonstrate the value of a new program or service which, if effective, can be incorporated into existing services for teens

WHAT is involved in writing a grant proposal

Research the funding sources
- Foundation and governmental sources can be tapped for planning and implementation grants.
- Make the initial contact with potential funders.

Write the proposal
- Follow the funder's directions; be sure to provide all the information requested.
- Write clearly and persuasively.

HOW to develop a grant proposal

There are two major steps in the development of a grant proposal — the search for a funder and the writing of the actual proposal.

The funding search

The first step in the funding search is to use the considerable number of resource guides available for this purpose. It is critical to know the target population, geographic limitations, types and size of grants, etc. of all the foundations in your area in order to match your library's good idea with a willing and appropriate funder. Some of the major resources include the following:
- *Guide to California's Foundations*
- *Foundation Directory*
- *Foundation Grants Index*
- *Taft Corporate Giving Directory*

For federal and state funding, the *Catalog of Federal Domestic Assistance* and the *Human Services Business Journal* are both useful references. There are also online databases listing foundations and grants, including at least two on DIALOG. Most major metropolitan areas have a foundation resource center.

After exploring the guides to determine possible funders, it is useful to follow up with a letter of inquiry and a telephone call or face-to-face conversation with foundation staff. This will alert you to changing funding priorities and funding cycles (see Appendix J for "Facts on Foundations"). Most proposals include several major components that are discussed below, although some funders only require the submission of a clearly written letter requesting support for small amounts.

In addition to the directories and guides, be aware of "requests for proposals" (RFPs) frequently issued from government or private sources which describe a service or program desired and solicit proposals from qualified contractors.

Writing the proposal

Proposal writing is both an art and a technique. The technical aspects of grant writing involve the ability to clearly articulate program goals and objectives that respond to an identified need. The more difficult and subtle side to grant writing is the capacity to identify and convince someone to fund a proposal. Many good ideas — and many well-written plans — are never funded. If a particular proposal is not funded, it can be recast to fit another funding source's requirements, while retaining the original service components.

Some general concepts to keep in mind when writing a proposal are listed below:

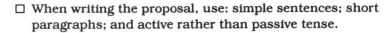

How-to Checklist: Writing a Proposal

☐ When writing the proposal, use: simple sentences; short paragraphs; and active rather than passive tense.

☐ Tailor your proposal for the funder. Write about the needs the funder wants to meet, and how your program will help meet them.

☐ Make sure the proposal is readable. Use easy-to-see, dark type. Break up the text with headings and subheadings.

☐ Number the pages and provide a table of contents if there are more than ten.

☐ Keep it simple. Assemble proposals neatly with paperclips and staples rather than using fancy bindings.

☐ Don't overwhelm the proposal with appendices. Make judicious use of relevant endorsements, news clippings, resumes, etc.

☐ Submit the proposal with a cover letter addressed to an individual. Never use "to whom it may concern." Verify spelling of names, addresses and titles.

The sections of a standard proposal are described below.

■ Proposal summary/abstract

The summary is one of the most important parts of a proposal. It is often the first section read by the funding source. It should be clear and concise and describe who you are, what you intend to do and how much money you are requesting.

■ Introduction

The introduction should attract the interest of the reader by highlighting in a dramatic fashion what problem or condition your project is responding to in the proposal. It should also clearly state what your library is going to do and make the case why the public library is in a position to do something about it. Establishing the public library's credibility in the introduction is critical to the success of the proposal.

■ Problem statement

The problem statement needs to be supported by data about youth at risk and make the case that something needs to be done about it. The challenge for the public library is to also demonstrate that the library can respond in a unique manner and do something about it that others cannot or are not doing. The problem or needs statement should not be confused with the next section which details what you are going to do and how you are going to do it. Also, the problem or need the library hopes to address should not be confused with the chronic lack of money to start a teen program. It should simply document the existence of a manageable problem in a clear and concise manner.

■ Program goals and objectives

The program goals and objectives should logically flow from the problem and state what the library hopes to accomplish and how it intends to do it. A goal is a broad statement of the general aim or thrust of a program. For example, a goal might be: "Increase the availability of information about current teen issues in a neighborhood." An objective, on the other hand, refers to more specific outcomes and might be: "During the next school year, eighty percent of all students in area high schools will have received a hip-pocket guide to all teen services in the county." This statement is both concrete and measurable. Goals and objectives are also discussed in Chapter IV, "Plan Development."

■ Methods

The methods section should describe what the library will do to reach the stated goals and objectives and why it picked one particular strategy over another. For example, the method for distributing the hip-pocket guide for teens can be premised on a traditional and effective outreach strategy already used by YA librarians — the booktalk visit to English classes in local junior high and high schools. This section should discuss the specific activities of a YA librarian and what s/he is going to do to meet the objectives described in previous sections.

■ Evaluation

The evaluation section should describe how the library program intends to measure whether it has reached any of its stated objectives. The evaluation can focus on outcomes (how many teens used the hip-pocket guides?) or on the process (how did the schools respond to the library outreach project?). For additional discussion on evaluation, see also Chapter IV and Chapter VI.

■ Future funding plans

This section should include a discussion of how the project being funded, if successful, will be incorporated into the ongoing operation of the library after the grant period ends. This should involve a substantive discussion of current library priorities and the possibility of restructuring existing services.

■ Budget and budget narrative

The budget is the flipside of the methods section. How much are each of the activities you have described going to cost? It should include a brief discussion of what each budget item will pay for in narrative form. The major categories usually include 1) personnel costs, 2) non-personnel costs, and 3) overhead. A sample budget

Figure 9. Sample Budget

	Req.	Donated	Total
I. PERSONNEL			
A. Salaries and Wages			
Project Coordinator @$2,000/month @100% x 12 months	24,000	0	24,000
2 Social Workers @$1,500/month each @50% time x 12 months	0	18,000	18,000
20 Volunteer Recreational Aides @50 hours each/year x 7.00/hour	0	7,000	7,000
B. Fringe Benefits			
20% of $42,000	4,800	3,600	8,400
C. Consultant and Contract Services			
Bookkeeping Services @$200/month x 12 months	0	2,400	2,400
Fundraising Services @$400/day x 10 days	4,000	0	4,000
Trainer @$250/day x 8 days	2,000	0	2,000
Annual Audit	2,000	2,000	4,000
II. NON-PERSONNEL			
A. Space			
900 square feet @$1.25/square foot/month x 12 months	13,500	0	13,500
Telephones @$200/month x 12 months	2,400	0	2,400
Utilities @$300/month x 12 months	0	3,600	3,600
Facility Insurance @$600/year	600	0	600
B. Rental, Lease, Purchase of Equipment			
Word processor/printer	2,000	0	2,000
12-passenger van @$400/month x 10 months	4,000	0	4,000
3 desk/chair sets @$250/each	750	0	750
C. Supplies			
Desk top supplies @$125/year/staff x 3	375	0	375
Educational materials @$50/month x 12 months	600	0	600
D. Travel			
4 roundtrip airfares LA-NY @$500/each	2,000	0	2,000
Reimbursement for staff auto travel @$.20/mile x avg of 400 miles/month x 12 months	960	0	960
8 days per diem (NY) @$150/day	1,200	0	1,200
E. Other Costs			
Conference Tuition (Creative Accounting) @$200/each x 4 staff	800	0	800
Board Liability Insurance	600	0	600
III. INDIRECT COSTS			
15.3% of TADC (Total Allowable Direct Costs) as per att. negot. rate with Dept. of Labor, 1988	10,860	0	10,860
TOTAL PROJECT COST:	**77,445**	**36,600**	**114,045**

is shown in Figure 9. For further discussion of the budget and budget narrative, see Chapter IV.

■ Appendix

The appendix often includes the following items:
- A financial statement
- List of governing board members
- Organizational chart
- Organization budget
- Timeline
- Letters of support
- Resumes and job descriptions
- Newspaper or journal articles on similar library projects

Letters of support can be very important, demonstrating community participation and a broad recognition of the need for your project. Such letters might ideally come from civic leaders who are familiar both with the library and with potential funders.

To solicit letters of support, write an open letter that includes your project title, mission and sufficient detail to assist and encourage your supporters to respond to your request. Be sure to include the name and address of the funding agency. A sample format for requesting letters of support is shown in Figure 10.

The quality of the presentation and format of all appendices, and the entire grant application, is very important. Make sure any photocopied material in appendices is clear and readable, as with the rest of the proposal. Use existing application forms, but add your own special touch to make your project stand out.

Figure 10. Request for Letters of Support

> Dear Library Supporter:
>
> I would like to ask you to write in support of an LSCA grant we have submitted to the State Library for $40,000 to fund our project, "Teaching Videos for Teens." If we are awarded the grant, the library will purchase 175 videos on various topics of interest to teens and in particular youth at risk, such as job-seeking skills, teen pregnancy, health and sexuality.
>
> Statistics demonstrate the necessity for librarians to address the needs of our population of youth at risk. In many libraries, the medium of video is a relatively new and popular service, attracting non-users and offering information in a different format. Among librarians, however, there is insufficient information about video collections.
>
> If funded, this project will gather and distribute information about educational videos for teens, including lists of titles and vendor sources; it will experiment with circulating these videos on interlibrary loan; and it will place a premiere collection of videos at the public library to evaluate use patterns and patron satisfaction.
>
> Please assist us by writing a letter by June 25, 1992 to the State Librarian (State Library, P.O. Box 0000, State Capitol) stating your support and giving at least one reason why you feel the community and libraries will benefit from project outcomes. Send the original to the State Librarian and a copy to me; of, if you prefer, give me the original and I will send it to the State Librarian. Thank you.
>
>
> Sincerely,
> Library Director

"I pretty much like doing everything. I like the variety."

— teen hired to work in a library under the BALIS YAR Project

Proposal Writing for the YAR Project

The initial idea for a YAR Project grew out of a recognition by members of the BALIS Children's Committee that library services for young adults were very limited in most Bay Area library systems and many problems among Bay Area youth were going un-addressed. They felt that each of the BALIS libraries should en-deavor to learn more about the needs of at-risk youth and share experiences about training approaches and innovative strategies used to expand and improve library services to teens.

To bring this idea to life, BALIS wrote a successful proposal for funding to the California State Library for a Library Services and Construction Act (LSCA) grant. BALIS had to conform to general requirements for submitting a proposal for LSCA funds.

Although a funding search was not needed for the project, the YAR Project Director did search for additional foundation support for the second year of the project in order to supplement funding for pilot projects in each of the nine library systems. Grants from two local foundations were secured.

Developing a Proposal

Background

Your library has just completed its needs assessment of youth at risk in your community and you have been asked to develop a service plan which reflects the priorities identified in the study. Your plan should include goals, objectives, staffing and budget, and be specific enough that it can be developed into a grant proposal for funding by an outside foundation.

Tasks

■ **Select a priority need among at-risk youth in your community to which your library can respond, given its mandate and strengths.**

■ **Develop a clear statement of purpose and program objectives for a YA service in your library that would meet this need.**

1. State one primary goal of your program.

2. Write two performance objectives which describe how your program will accomplish its primary goal. Write specific, measurable objectives which assign accountability and a deadline for the task.

■ **Identify possible funding sources for the program you are proposing.**

1. Which corporate sponsor or local foundation would be interested in funding library services for youth at risk? Consult a guide to foundations if available.

2. How can the library program you are developing be made attractive to potential funders?

CHAPTER VI. Program Evaluation

Evaluation is an essential component of any library program. It should be built into the planning process at an early stage and become an integral part of further program development. Evaluation can help answer questions about which strategies for delivering library services to teens work best, and why. This is true for both new and existing library services.

The public sector has entered a period of accountability where resources are scarce and the need to assess the effectiveness and efficiency of all programs remains critical. This is especially true in the area of youth services where full support is not always sufficient in the legislative and budgetary arena. Therefore, it is even more incumbent upon library staff to carefully document the impact of YA programs on the teen population they serve and publicize their successes.

WHY evaluate programs for youth at risk

- To determine whether the programs are working and whether they are an effective and efficient use of library resources
- To identify areas for improvement and change
- To document success in order to build administrative and community support and ensure ongoing funding

WHAT a librarian should do to evaluate programs for youth at risk

For both new and current library services, the first task of an evaluator is to identify major programmatic goals and objectives of all YA services or selected components. It is also important to identify the target audience for services. Each objective should specify desired outcomes and can then be posed as a researchable evaluative question. YA program evaluation questions might include the following:

- What is the quality and quantity of YA services currently being offered in your library?
- Are YA programs reaching the teens they were meant to serve? Are they reaching youth at risk?
- Are YA programs having any measurable impact on the lives of teens being served?

The research process that will help answer evaluation questions can be brief and anecdotal or involve a more extensive research design which examines YA programs more systematically and monitors and assesses their activities and impacts on youth at risk over time. This will require a staff member (or an outside consultant) to address these tasks:

- Clearly define what is to be evaluated
- Develop an appropriate evaluation design
- Determine output measures and data collection methods
- Analyze data and implement findings

HOW to evaluate programs for youth at risk

Define what needs evaluation

An evaluator needs to determine what program (or component of a program) should be the major focus of the evaluation study and which goals and objectives need to be targeted. If there is a clear consensus on major goals and objectives (see Chapter IV, "Plan Development" and Chapter V, "Proposal Writing"), it will be easier to develop specific evaluation questions and a research design which can answer them.

If, for example, a program objective states that YA staff will do community outreach by conducting booktalks in English classes at three local high schools, then the research question might be:

- How many booktalks were conducted during the fall semester?
- How many students who heard the booktalks are utilizing the public library?
- How many students who heard the booktalks have improved their English course grades?

The more ambitious the program goals and objectives (as in the question about grades above), the more ambitious the research design and data collection methods need to be. The evaluator will have to make choices about how extensive the study will be based on an assessment of his/her own time and resource constraints.

Develop an appropriate evaluation design

For an evaluation study to go beyond the basic question of whether a specific program accomplished its major tasks (e.g., visited the neighborhood high school and conducted the promised number of booktalks), the research design would have to include "before and after" measures (for example, library utilization rates or student grades prior to and after the series of high school booktalks) as well as the same data (library utilization rates and student grades) from a comparison group. A comparison group might consist of a sample of teens at a similar high school where no booktalks were held. This would allow the evaluator to answer the more important question about the impact of the booktalks on library use or grades. Figure 11 illustrates this comparison group design using the English grade point average as one criterion of "success" (with some hypothetical findings and a dose of wishful thinking!).

Figure 11. Table Illustrating Booktalk Program Impact

	English Grade Point Average **Before** Booktalk Programs	English Grade Point Average **After** Booktalk Programs
Group 1: Students Receiving Booktalks	2.3	3.1
Group 2: Students Not Receiving Booktalks	2.4	2.5

Many evaluation research designs do not include comparison groups or "before and after" data. All designs, however, should include the components listed below.

How-to Checklist: Designing an Evaluation

☐ Include a set of research questions for the evaluation study.

☐ Outline a method of selecting a sample of programs or respondents for study, if possible with a comparison group.

☐ Incorporate a plan for identifying and collecting data on "output" measures, if possible, both before and after the date a YAR program has been in effect.

☐ Include a plan for analyzing and disseminating the findings.

Determine outcome measures and data collection methods

Outcome measures need to be linked to the YAR program objectives and easy to define and collect. They might include the following:

- YA utilization (number of reference requests, library cards, etc.)
- Special teen programs (number of teen participants, satisfaction scores, etc.)
- Community outreach (number of school visits, collaborative projects, flyers distributed, etc.)

- YA staff support for teen programs
- School performance of library users (grades, drop-out rates, etc.)

The American Library Association has published a book on *Output Measures for Public Library Services to Children* (1992) which covers in great detail more standardized procedures for collecting data on library services for children. A more complete list of suggested indicators for the YAR Project is included in Appendix K.

The next step is to decide how to collect the data which will answer the evaluation questions. This can involve a very simple research design or a more complicated one. Evidence of program success can come from anecdotal information obtained through observation or interview. It can also come from a more elaborate survey of attitudes and opinions from large numbers of people coupled with supporting statistical data documenting program impacts in the library and/or in the community.

Analyze data and implement findings

Data analysis techniques will allow the researcher to tally the results of study and assess the degree of success or failure of a program. Qualitative data can be summarized in narrative form, while presentation of quantitative data usually requires the use of statistics in tables, charts, and/or graphs.

Results should be utilized by library managers and staff to develop and improve services to youth at risk. Plans for dissemination outside the library will vary depending on the audience for the evaluation study.

Evaluation of the YAR Project

CASE EXAMPLE

The YAR Project was evaluated in its second year by an outside consultant who designed an evaluation plan for a selected number of the YAR pilot projects in each of the nine participating libraries. During the planning process each library was asked to prepare a clear set of goals and objectives that helped guide the evaluation. Project staff, in consultation with YAR Project Steering Committee members, also developed a list of possible indicators of success which were incorporated into the evaluation design.

The outside consultant proposed an evaluation process which included a series of meetings with library staff to help shape an appropriate research design. Thus, the resulting designs included input from those directly involved in the planning and program development process.

The consultant visited each site and identified four major categories of output measures — increased library use by teens, development of special teen programs and tutoring programs, and expansion of teen collections and facilities. Several data collection methods were developed for all the sites, including interviews, head counts, observations, etc.

> "There's plenty there in the library. Kids just don't know about it."
>
> — *Oakland teen*

The consultant's original design for the evaluation of the YAR projects emphasized the impact of the library programs on youth at risk. The intent was to document how the provision of focused library services improved the well-being of the population targeted. In addition, the evaluation would describe the activities of all nine of the participating libraries, but concentrate on measuring user impact at only three of the sites. The sites were to be selected on the basis of the innovation and replicability of their programs. The methods that were to be used included the following:

- *Focus groups*
- *Surveys*
- *Interviews*
- *Participant observation*
- *Analysis of secondary data*

After some preliminary analysis, the consultants concluded that the data necessary for this evaluation design were unavailable, for the most part. After this realization, the project design moved away from documenting the impact of the YAR programs on such indicators as youth use of the library and the circulation of YA materials. The evaluation shifted its focus more to the identification of organizational models for YAR programs. The final version of the evaluation therefore devotes more attention to describing the process of creating YAR programs and less attention to attempting to measure their impact.

There were two principal methods used to conduct the evaluation. The first was interviews with library staff at each of the nine participating libraries. Staff were interviewed at least three times during the project: at the start of the implementation phase, midway through implementation and at the conclusion of this phase. At the concluding session, the consultant also interviewed the head librarian as well as YA staff.

The second data collection method was observation of as many of the youth programs and community outreach activities as possible during the period of the evaluation. When feasible, this observation included interviews with youth attending the event. Since most of the events were not formally structured, a written user survey could not be effectively employed. The information obtained in this way was largely opportunistic and anecdotal due to the developmental nature of the YAR program at most of the sites.

Evaluating Program Effectiveness

Background

You have been asked to evaluate YAR services in your library system. Several services (paperback rack, booktalks, etc.) are currently being offered for young adults. There is a difference of opinion among staff about which ones are most effective in reaching a teen audience in your community. There is also some new funding available ($5,000/year for the next five years) for expanded services to youth at risk, which was donated by a wealthy patron for that specific purpose.

Tasks

■ **Clearly state the major goals and objectives of at least one teen program component in your library system.**

■ **Develop outcome measures which provide information on whether or not the teen program has made measurable progress toward reaching its goals.**

1. How would you measure whether the program is providing the services which it set out to provide?

2. Develop two indicators and methods (participation rates, survey/interview, observation) for measuring both the quality and quantity of the teen program.

3. How would you measure whether the program is having an impact on the teen population you are serving?

4. Develop two indicators and methods (survey/interview, secondary data, etc.) for measuring the impact the program has had on teens in the community (test scores, drop-out rates, etc.)

■ **Match the results of the evaluation with the needs that were identified during the assessment phase.**

1. Has the project met the need?

2. What is the next step? Given the $5,000/year donation for the next five years, how would the funds best be used to meet the needs of youth at risk in your community?

CHAPTER VII.

Multicultural/Multiethnic Library Services for Youth

This guidebook grew out of a project undertaken in California, where demographic shifts have made communities increasingly multiethnic. Some California communities are already more than fifty percent non-white, shifting areas of the state to a population dynamic in which no single ethnic group has a majority.

These demographic shifts will continue in California as well as in other parts of the country, and often are seen in younger age groups first. But these changes are not unique to youth. They will affect all of us at all ages and will be an issue for the nation.

All library services must address this change or risk alienating a growing portion of the community. In the case of services to at-risk youth, this is particularly important. As a group, children and youth may be more ethnically diverse than the community at large, and need active encouragement to use the library.

Especially in light of our nation's changing demography, then, it is critical for librarians to be knowledgeable of and sensitive to the needs of an increasingly multicultural and multiethnic society. This is absolutely essential to the development of successful and culturally appropriate library programs for teens.

WHY develop multicultural/ multiethnic youth services

- To respond to the growing cultural and ethnic diversity among youth since, in some areas of the country, the percentage of ethnic groups is much higher among those under eighteen years of age than in the general population

- To respond to the critical needs of ethnic youth who tend to be at greatest risk of a wide range of health and social problems and who need a user-friendly, neighborhood-based, and non-judgmental source of information
- To reach out to teens who are at a crucial age in terms of self-identity and need to have their own cultural roots and traditions reflected in the services libraries offer

WHAT a librarian should do to work effectively in a multicultural/ multiethnic community

Develop library collections reflecting the multiethnic and multicultural population
- Expand a collection of YA library materials that reflects the ethnic and cultural diversity of the population served.
- Display library materials and use bilingual signs/posters in the YA area that reflect the ethnic and cultural diversity of the population served.

Recruit culturally and ethnically diverse staff
- Work with library associations, library schools and staff to promote culturally and ethnically diverse enrollment in library schools and encourage a diverse group of students to specialize in the young adult field.
- Encourage the placement of culturally and ethnically diverse staff in library programs for teens.

Provide staff training on multiculturalism
- Develop staff training sessions on specific ethnic and cultural groups being served and how libraries need to respond to changing communities.
- Develop a series of workshops devoted to cultural sensitivity.

Develop programs which focus on cultural identity
- Convene youth advisory groups and create linkages with a broad range of community organizations to gather input on collection development and youth programming.
- Highlight programs and materials that reflect cultural roots, interests and heroes.

HOW to work effectively with youth in a multicultural/ multiethnic community

In addition to developing a more diverse collection of library materials, librarians and other staff need to make a conscious effort to sensitize themselves to the growing diversity among the teens they serve. Active participation in cultural sensitivity trainings is one way for library staff to begin to examine more closely their own attitudes about race and ethnicity as well as foster some creative thinking about the way teens from various cultural backgrounds are currently being served. Some of the other actions librarians can take are listed below.

How-to Checklist: Developing Multicultural/ Multiethnic Youth Services

☐ Review and assess the availability of bilingual and culturally diverse materials for YAs. Look around at local bookstores in multicultural neighborhoods, talk to community ethnic or cultural organizations, and network with library organizations like ALA's Ethnic Materials Information Exchange (EMIE).

☐ Develop collections of ethnic materials as needed for YAs.

☐ Design library displays (signs, posters, etc.) in the YA section which highlight ethnic traditions and cultural heroes.

☐ Conduct cultural sensitivity training sessions for all library staff.

☐ Recruit a culturally diverse staff or youth volunteers who reflect the population served in the community.

☐ Form a youth advisory committee or task force on cultural issues.

☐ Hold a series of ethnic programs oriented to teenagers (youth forums, rap sessions, etc.).

☐ Develop an outreach program in schools and other youth-serving agencies which emphasizes the contributions of specific cultural groups to the community.

☐ Request assistance from other libraries that have developed expertise with multiethnic/multicultural materials and services.

☐ Look for and use training tapes, consultants and/or expert staff from other libraries to help develop staff training programs on multicultural topics.

CASE EXAMPLE

Multicultural Services in the YAR Project

In conducting needs assessment studies in each of the nine BALIS libraries, it was essential to understand the needs of youth across a broad range of diverse cultural groups. In the planning and needs assessment phase of the YAR Project, every effort was made to ensure that local YAR teams were representative of the major ethnic groups in their communities.

Several of the libraries highlighted the special needs of a specific ethnic group in their needs assessment study. African-American youth in San Francisco and Oakland, for example, became the prime focus of outreach and tutoring programs in high-risk neighborhoods in both cities.

In Contra Costa County, a choice was made to focus on the needs of recent Asian immigrants in the San Pablo area. Contacts were made during and after the needs assessment process with local community-based organizations serving Asian youth. Through one CBO, the library helped a group of Laotian refugee youth start a T-shirt business, Young Asian Entrepreneurs (YAE). One result: when county government considered budget cuts for the library, YAE sent a testimonial letter to a county supervisor stating that "without the help of the San Pablo Library, YAE would never have happened and we would all be out on the street without much to strive for."

"Without the help of the San Pablo Library YAE would never have happened and we would all be out on the street without much to strive for."

— teen entrepreneur, after getting help from the library in establishing a business

The San Pablo Branch also developed a collection of culturally-appropriate video materials. Similar programs may be implemented in other parts of the county based on the success of this model program.

During the first year of the YAR Project, a sensitivity training session was held for all project staff. Several local libraries later sponsored similar sensitivity training programs for their own staff.

Developing Multicultural Public Library Services for Youth

Background

You have been asked to develop a series of library programs for teens in your multicultural and multiethnic community. There is a fairly good collection of materials for different ethnic groups, but use of these materials is very low, especially among young people.

Tasks

■ Identify an appropriate strategy for increasing utilization of the library by at least one ethnic group in your community. Develop an outreach strategy which might help improve the library's image as a user-friendly institution in that community.

■ Develop a list of workshops for your staff which would improve the awareness and sensitivity of the cultural background of one ethnic group in your area.

■ Develop a list of five things you can do to make the physical layout and displays in your branch more user friendly to ethnic youth.

■ Develop a strategy for finding out about ethnic youth needs and interests in your community and suggest how you might develop a YA program that responds to the needs of at least one ethnic group.

CHAPTER VIII. # Staff Training

Positive attitudes towards teenagers in society, a basic understanding about adolescence as a critical developmental stage, and up-to-date knowledge about the major issues facing teens today are all key components to working effectively with youth. A series of workshops for all library staff that come into contact with teens should become an integral part of the staff development curriculum.

WHY learn about youth at risk

- To increase understanding of the important and distinct developmental stages of children and adolescents
- To increase understanding of contemporary youth-related issues
- To learn techniques for effectively working and communicating with youth
- To understand and access the increasingly complex network of public and non-profit services for youth
- To be able to plan and provide public library service that is relevant to the needs of local youth

WHAT training is needed to serve youth at risk

Use both passive and active learning
- Use passive learning — formal presentations — to directly pass on information on specific topics.
- Use active learning — a more interactive style — to provide training in skill-related subjects.
- Involve all library staff (including clerks, security guards, etc.) who come into contact with teen patrons.

Give information on key teen issues
- Conduct forums or discussion groups on psychosocial and developmental issues during adolescence.
- Present information describing the network of youth services in your area.
- Develop programs for staff dealing with contemporary teen problems/concerns/language/culture.

Build confidence for working with teens from diverse backgrounds
- Teach communication skills.
- Encourage development of cultural sensitivity.

HOW to organize trainings about youth at risk

A successful youth at risk training program requires clear goals for each workshop, qualified and effective presenters, good publicity and attention to logistical details (see the How-to Checklist: Preparing a Workshop, later in this chapter).

There are five major phases involved in the organization of a training program:

How-to Checklist: Organizing a Training Program

□ Conduct a brief needs assessment of perceived training needs among library staff.

□ Develop a series of well-planned workshops using both hands-on and lecture formats.

□ Identify qualified and capable workshop presenters who are willing to adapt their training materials to the needs of library participants.

□ Publicize workshops to let interested staff know the time, place, registration process, and the importance of training on youth at risk issues.

□ Evaluate each workshop as well as the overall impact of the training on the quality of library services to youth.

Assess training needs

A prerequisite for effective training is the willing participation of those involved. Management support is essential. There also needs to be some recognition among library staff that they will benefit from a youth at risk workshop. Thus, in the planning phase, the organizer should marshall administrative and staff support to maximize attendance and benefits from the workshop. This may entail the following tasks:

- Meeting with managers, librarians, and Friends of the Library groups to get their input and support
- Raising funds to pay for speakers (unless this is covered by staff development budget or fees)
- Meeting with youth and experts in the field to help shape the workshop agendas
- Reading available materials on contemporary youth issues

Design the training program

For the most effective program, workshop topics should include:

- A developmental perspective on adolescence (i.e., independence/autonomy issue, physiological changes, sexuality, peer group influence, etc.)
- An overview of the formal and informal networks for teens in the community
- A description of at-risk behaviors among teens
- A description of the current network of services for youth along with a discussion of innovative strategies and model programs for reducing the negative consequences of at-risk behavior
- A presentation on a specific theme or problem among teens
- Sensitivity training on issues of race, gender, sexual orientation
- Practical training on communication skills with teens
- Teen program development (planning, budgeting, publicizing, evaluating library services for youth, etc.)
- YA programming ideas and collection development
- Effective videos and/or other audiovisual tools to add variety to the training program format

Find qualified and effective presenters

Finding the right person requires some good luck and intuition, but the recommendation of those who have seen a speaker in action is a useful guide. Some of the resources for locating affordable and available presenters are listed below:

- Local colleges and universities
- Speaker's bureaus
- Youth service providers (teen clinics, drug treatment programs, schools, etc.)
- Local teen organizations, clubs, programs (student body leaders, teens in recovery in drug treatment programs, etc.)

If at all possible, involve teens themselves in the planning of the training and, if possible, in the workshop itself.

Determine the most effective presentation style for the intended audience. It can vary from a formal lecture presentation to small group interactional exercises with role-play and modelling by the speaker. Presenters can also use a case study approach or draw on more general material. The presentation might incorporate the use of the following training tools:

- Written handouts to participants (sent out in advance if possible)
- Flipcharts and/or chalkboards for recording
- Audiovisual presentations (videotape, slides, etc.)
- Panels and/or individual presentations
- Interactive exercises in small groups
- The use of a group facilitator to brainstorm, build group consensus, etc.

Publicize

Think about the intended audiences for the workshop and how their work will be easier or more productive as a result of learning these facts and skills. Then write flyers and announcements for staff newsletters/bulletins and staff meetings (see examples from YAR Project trainings in Appendix L). Be sure to include who, what, where, when, why and how much (if there is a cost involved).

Evaluate the success and impact of the workshop

The use of a workshop participant questionnaire is the most common and efficient method of evaluating a training. Ask the participants to evaluate the material and the presenter. Also ask them to rate the overall usefulness of the workshop (see sample in Figure 12). If possible, a follow-up survey or observational study should be conducted several months after the workshop to assess its sustained value. Library patrons and staff supervisors can also be surveyed to comment more objectively on any programmatic and behavioral changes perceived among those who attended a workshop.

Figure 12. Sample Workshop Evaluation Form

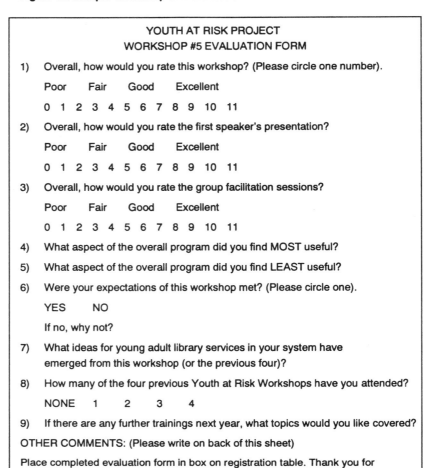

YOUTH AT RISK PROJECT
WORKSHOP #5 EVALUATION FORM

1) Overall, how would you rate this workshop? (Please circle one number).

   Poor   Fair   Good   Excellent

   0 1 2 3 4 5 6 7 8 9 10 11

2) Overall, how would you rate the first speaker's presentation?

   Poor   Fair   Good   Excellent

   0 1 2 3 4 5 6 7 8 9 10 11

3) Overall, how would you rate the group facilitation sessions?

   Poor   Fair   Good   Excellent

   0 1 2 3 4 5 6 7 8 9 10 11

4) What aspect of the overall program did you find MOST useful?

5) What aspect of the overall program did you find LEAST useful?

6) Were your expectations of this workshop met? (Please circle one).

   YES   NO

   If no, why not?

7) What ideas for young adult library services in your system have emerged from this workshop (or the previous four)?

8) How many of the four previous Youth at Risk Workshops have you attended?

   NONE   1   2   3   4

9) If there are any further trainings next year, what topics would you like covered?

OTHER COMMENTS: (Please write on back of this sheet)

Place completed evaluation form in box on registration table. Thank you for attending.

Attention to detail

Checklists can be particularly helpful in keeping track of the many planning and logistical details involved in preparing for a workshop. The following list includes the tasks involved in preparing for most workshops.

How-to Checklist: Preparing a Workshop

☐ Conduct a brief assessment of training needs among library staff.

☐ Obtain management approval for the workshop.

☐ Contact the library manager and staff development staff about the workshop.

☐ Develop a workshop budget.

☐ Determine funding arrangements (grant, fees, etc.).

☐ Develop a list of possible speakers.

☐ Contact the list of proposed speakers by phone.

☐ Discuss the purpose of the workshop with each speaker (in person or by phone).

☐ Confirm speaker arrangements in writing.

☐ Determine each speaker's room layout and audiovisual needs.

☐ Research possible sites for the workshop.

☐ Visit sites (for space, chairs, etc.).

☐ Finalize arrangements and reserve room(s).

☐ Develop publicity materials and a strategy for their dissemination.

☐ Conduct publicity and outreach to all potential participants.

☐ Make arrangements for coffee, refreshments, and/or lunch.

☐ Reserve necessary audiovisual equipment.

☐ Make signs, name tags, etc.

☐ Develop a registration procedure.

☐ Identify and prepare all handout materials.

☐ Develop a workshop agenda and an evaluation form.

CASE EXAMPLE

Workshops for the YAR Project

The YAR Project convened a series of workshops on youth at risk issues for all library staff in the San Francisco Bay Area during the winter and spring of 1991. The topics were selected after consultation with the YAR Steering Committee made up of YA librarians and/or library directors representing all nine BALIS libraries.

The topics selected included the following:
- ***Bay Area Youth — At Risk of What and Why?*** *(plus a special skills workshop on communicating with teens)*
- ***The Youth-Serving Network —Politics and Programs***
- ***Librarians — What Have You Done For Me Lately! (A Youth Speakout)***
- ***Cross-Cultural Issues and Youth***
- ***"Turning the Corner" for YAR — Implementing YA Services in Public Libraries***

There were additional training sessions for small groups of library staff on two other topics:
- ***Plan Writing and Budget Development for YAR Pilot Projects***
- ***Evaluating YA Services***

"When working with teens, refreshments are a top priority!"

— librarian working on the BALIS YAR Project

All trainings were held at public library meeting rooms and were half day morning sessions. Most participants registered in advance and attendance averaged seventy-five at each session. There was a nominal registration fee which covered the cost of refreshments served during the breaks.

Presenters were selected on the basis of their background and knowledge of youth issues and a willingness to adapt their material to the needs of the audience. The project director developed the topics and worked with each presenter to shape the presentation to the needs of the library audience. The workshops on the network of services and the youth speakout used a panel format. The presentations on the meaning of being "at risk" and cross-cultural issues were followed by facilitated sessions on communication skills and multiculturalism. The workshop on YA services implementation was led by an experienced facilitator and involved the use of group brainstorming exercises.

Publicity was developed with flyers and a calendar prepared by the BALIS staff development coordinator. Videotaping was arranged for most of the sessions and one of the workshops was recorded live by a local cable TV station as well as public radio for later airing. Some of the tapes have been requested for use by local libraries for additional staff training.

Each workshop was evaluated by participants through the use of a written questionnaire. The formal feedback along with advice from the YAR Steering Committee helped shape each of the training sessions.

Staff Training — Tooling Up for Working with Teens

Background

Both professional and support staff in your library system have asked for skill development and training opportunities to help them cope with the teenagers who are coming into the library. You have been asked to put together a series of workshops on youth issues.

Tasks

■ **Identify topics for library and support staff on youth at risk issues.**

1. List and prioritize five topics on problems and programs affecting youth in your community which your library staff need to know more about.

2. List and prioritize five skill areas needed by library staff to work more effectively with teenagers.

■ **Identify possible speakers for the workshop series and what teaching methods would be most effective in presenting information on youth issues.**

1. List five resources (organizations or individuals) in your area who might have or recommend presenters for your training sessions.

2. Select three topics and match each one with a preferred teaching method (lecture, experiential, panel, etc.).

CHAPTER IX.   # Public Relations and Publicity

Library services and special events which focus on youth issues can effectively focus community attention on the public library. A public relations campaign about library service targeted at children and youth can help create a positive image of the public library.

Even though getting access to the print and broadcast media may be somewhat difficult, media exposure is increasingly becoming the most effective method to raise awareness in your community about innovative library services to an at-risk population. Public relations differ from publicity about a specific event although the two should be coordinated whenever possible.

WHY conduct public relations and publicity campaigns

- To raise awareness among the public and their elected officials of the library's critical role in serving this vulnerable group
- To reach at-risk youth and their families with information about programs specially designed for teens
- To increase utilization of teen services among at-risk youth who are not currently using library services
- To inform at-risk teens of specific events and programs

WHAT a librarian should do for public relations and publicity

Public relations
- Design a public relations strategy that includes an overall theme appealing to teens and the media.
- Create a series of ads and/or public service announcements (PSAs) about your library's concern for children and youth.
- Develop and publicize newsworthy special events and programs for teens.

Teen program publicity
- Prepare user-friendly publicity materials about general YA services and specific programs the library offers for teens in your community (see Appendix M for a sample).
- Use existing communication channels whenever available in the community and through the schools.

HOW to conduct public relations and publicity for youth at risk

Design a public relations theme

Public libraries need consistent and positive media coverage of their role in responding to topical issues on the public agenda. This often entails a long-term commitment to work with the media on the library's general contributions to the community and a free society. To gain attention and public recognition of the library's focus on youth, develop a logo (visual) and slogan (audio) which conveys in an instant the library's focus on serving this at-risk population. Use that theme in all written communications with the media to raise awareness of your program and your message.

Create a public relations program

Librarians should read, listen and watch a wide variety of media outlets to determine which reporters and stations or newspapers are interested in at-risk youth. Notice what types of talk shows, regular features, reader's columns, or bulletin boards are available. Then outline a program that will reach your target audiences in a regular, planned way. This will let them know that the library is doing something for youth in your community. Comments from an advisory group can be an important source of community input for such an effort.

Public service announcements

Ad campaigns, free speech messages, and public service announcements (PSAs) are all effective tools in a public relations program. Figure 13 shows a sample PSA. Whenever possible, continue to use a consistent slogan and logo to raise the recognition factor among the public.

Network affiliates, local TV and radio stations and cable TV each have their own policies with regard to community access to the airwaves for PSAs and free speech messages. Some will accept tapes, while others will make their studios available for taping and production. Often, the station's own anchorperson, disk jockey or personality will read your prepared message. Research all these possibilities through telephone calls to the community affairs directors of selected local stations.

Figure 13. Public Service Announcement Sample

Free Speech Message Text: KTVU - Channel 2, Oakland

It's 3 o'clock! Do you know where your teenage son or daughter is?

Well, thanks to the public libraries in Alameda, Contra Costa and San Francisco counties, the chances that they are involved in programs at the public library are greater than they were a year ago.

That's because of a series of new programs at local libraries for teens around the Bay Area. They include outreach to schools and community centers, rap sessions, special forums on jobs and cultural issues, and a new tutoring program for teens at the MLK Branch of the Oakland Public Library.

Public libraries are a free, neighborhood-based, and safe place for kids to find teen magazines, tapes, books, get their homework assignments done, **AND** hook into other programs designed especially for them. They are a **proven** network of **preventive** services for youth.

Contact your local library and other active youth-serving agencies to find out ways **YOU** can help at-risk teens in your community.

[Aired during month of April, 1992 in the San Francisco Bay Area]

Create an event

You can also capture media attention by "creating an event" which the media will cover. This approach requires developing an idea or concept which appeals to a news director at a local TV or radio station or newspaper.

The major challenge is deciding on what is a "newsworthy event" and how to package your message. Some ideas for making such a determination are listed below:
- Selecting the right time (for example, when school opens in fall)
- Building on a topical issue (teens and AIDS)
- Releasing a report on a teen-related topic
- Collaborating with another organization planning an event

Several steps will help increase your chances of getting your event covered:

How-to Checklist: Creating a Public Relations Event

☐ Decide on a descriptive and topical theme.

☐ Write a clear and concise press release.

☐ Develop a current media list with contact names.

☐ Set up a convenient and photogenic time/place (steps of City Hall, a local school or public library, etc.).

☐ Place follow-up calls to key media contacts.

Publicize programs

Publicity is critical to the success of teen programs. Librarians need to get the word out to the right people, in the right way, and in a timely manner. By being creative and involving teens in the development of publicity materials and outreach strategies for YA programs, the chances of success will increase considerably. Figures 14 and 15 show samples of general YA publicity.

Some tips that will help in conducting successful publicity are listed below.

How-to Checklist: Publicizing Programs

☐ Consult with a group of teens in an informal focus group or advisory committee to find out the best means for reaching their peers with information about library programs.

☐ Consider a broad range of media strategies (e.g. flyers/posters, radio/TV spots, oral presentations in school and other community settings, outreach to parents and teachers as well as the teens themselves).

☐ Whenever possible, use existing communication channels which already have a successful track record in reaching teens (e.g., school newspapers, recreation center bulletin boards, local teen TV cable stations or radio shows).

☐ Develop flyers/posters and scripts about YA services and specific teen programs you are developing for discussion and trial use.

☐ Use terminology and images which are colorful, catchy and current and incorporate teen jargon (e.g. "teen", not "YA" services; "s'up?" rather than "what's going on?").

☐ Use the youth-serving network and the local schools to publicize library services for teens and to get your message out.

☐ Always follow up with a phone call to make sure your publicity materials were received and were posted or distributed.

☐ Offer to present your information at events teens are likely to attend (e.g., school assemblies, sporting events).

☐ Call the producers and/or hosts of popular local teen radio and TV shows to offer to be a guest.

☐ Publicize your program to elected officials. Ask to be included on meeting agendas to announce grant awards and/or present project materials to local boards and councils. Bringing teens along is a good way to get directly into the local paper.

Figure 14. Sample Bookcover Graphics

Knowledge

Power

p.m.
i.m. to 5:30 p.m.

Use It!

Important Numbers:

Planned Parenthood
482 West MacArthur, Oakland
652-7526

Adult Literacy Program 865-2454

Xanthos (Counseling and Rap Groups)
1335 Park Ave., Alameda
522-8363

Alameda Recreation and Park Department
Santa Clara and Oak
748-4565

Alameda Public Health Center
2226 Santa Clara Ave, Alameda
522-0889

Emergency 911

AC Transit 839-2882

Aids Hotline
English/ Spanish 1-800-367-2437
Filipino 1-800-345-2435

Suicide Prevention - Alameda County
849-2212

Your important numbers:

_____
_____
_____
_____
_____

Figure 15. Sample Bookmark Graphics

WHAT'S IN IT FOR YOU?

Information for school and life

Stuff to read, watch, hear, and use

books
tapes
cd's
typewriter
public computer

Livermore Public Library

a safe place

OPEN EVERY DAY

Civic Center Branch
1000 S. Livermore Ave.
Mon-Thur 10-9
Fri & Sat 10-5
Sunday 1-5

Springtown Branch
998 Bluebell Dr
Tue & Thur 10-6
Wednesday 1-8
Saturday 10-5

Publicity and Public Relations in the YAR Project

The Oakland Public Library effectively used various media strategies to publicize the opening of its tutoring center at the Martin Luther King, Jr. Branch. The library produced flyers to recruit students and volunteer tutors, which were distributed to all local agencies and schools. The Oakland Volunteer Bureau helped publicize the need for tutors (see Appendix N). Local schools (there are two within a block of the MLK Branch) and churches were also contacted about the new tutoring center.

As the project opened, the library's public information officer obtained local newspaper and cable TV coverage and an editorial in the major Oakland newspaper. The manager of the MLK Branch and the YAR Project director also appeared on a local cable TV show in which the overall project and the tutoring center were discussed.

In addition to the local publicity efforts about YAR programs in each of the nine participating library systems — which included flyers, newspaper ads, PSAs, community calendar listings on local radio and television — the YAR Project developed a publicity strategy for the entire Bay Area media market.

This process started with the recognition that the project needed some credibility in non-library circles. In addition to the needs assessment teams that were convened in each site, a YAR Project Advisory Committee was formed. It consisted of prominent individuals who had name recognition in each of the communities involved in the project. A project logo was used on project stationery, and prominently displayed on all meeting flyers and agendas, training materials, and project reports.

Once these tasks were accomplished, the publicity efforts that followed were more likely to succeed. They included the following components:

Press conference

- *A press conference was called at a "newsworthy" moment in the two-year project (see Appendix O). This occurred after the needs assessments were completed and the action plans were about to be released.*
- *A press packet was assembled which included a press release summarizing the key points in a few punchy sentences. The packet included a one-page summary of all the YAR pilot projects about to be launched along with some demographic information on at-risk teens in each of the nine communities.*
- *The press conference was held mid-morning at a convenient location for local press. The California State Librarian and a well-known YA author spoke before the nine YAR plans for service were unveiled and released to the public.*

Use of video

- *A project video was compiled utilizing TV news coverage footage as well as training tapes from the YAR workshops. Some interviews with participating librarians were also taped and included in the video.*

- *A local video production firm was also retained to develop three rap public service announcements (PSAs). The three PSAs were based on three of the themes which had surfaced in the needs assessment phase of the project (jobs, cultural roots, and STDs). The key line in the rap song used was, "Knowledge...POWER...Use It!" The music was written and performed by a local rapper (Chill E. B.) and a multiethnic group of dancers. The PSAs were distributed and played locally on several network and cable TV stations during the second year of the YAR Project.*

Use of local media

- *Ads on teens and the library were designed and placed in several youth publications, including high school newspapers (see Figure 16).*

- *Several local newspapers and TV stations covered events held as part of the YAR Project, including airing of one of the trainings on public radio and a local cable TV station.*

- *Lead stories and editorials appeared in several major daily newspapers, covering both specific events (as in Figure 17) and the YAR Project in general (as in Figure 18).*

Other strategies

- *T-shirts were donated by a local foundation and silk-screened by a homeless youth program in San Francisco. The T-shirts had the project logo on the front and the PSA message on the back. They were distributed throughout the Bay Area to youth participants in the YAR programs.*

- *An article on the project was submitted for publication in a professional journal for librarians.*

- *Several panel presentations were made at local, statewide, and national library conferences throughout the course of the project (see Appendix P).*

Figure 16. Sample Newspaper Ad

Contest: Querying a librarian

San Lorenzo students try to baffle visiting librarians with an array of tricky questions.

YOU ASKED WHAT?

■ The San Lorenzo library sponsors a fun competition for high school students

By Marilee Strong
STAFF WRITER

SAN LORENZO — Did you ever wonder how many full-grown male pit bulls one could squeeze into Newark's 10-story Hilton Hotel? What Jose Canseco's mom's name is? Or what makes people's feet stink?

San Lorenzo High School students have. Since Wednesday their inquiring minds have worked overtime in an attempt to stump a team of visiting librarians with questions ranging from the profound to the mundane to the imponderable.

The three-day "Stump the Librarian" contest at the high school is the first in a series of projects sponsored by the San Lorenzo Public Library under a youth-at-risk grant to show young people what resources libraries have to offer.

"We want young people to realize that libraries are not just useful for homework assignments but a place to go to for non-judgmental answers on anything from helping them look for a summer job or finding out where to get support for a personal family problem to information about sex or birth control and AIDS, or drugs and alcohol," said library manager Judy Flum.

In May and June the public library will hold a series of six youth forums on the areas a needs study showed young people most want information about: jobs and job skills, multi-cultural relations, and health and sexuality.

But first the librarians decided to

stage a fun event at the high school to help break down the stereotype of libraries as the domain of the uncool.

With a pizza party offered as a prize to the fourth-period class to most often stump the librarians, students mobbed the table the librarians set up outside the cafeteria with questions only a teen-age mind could fully appreciate.

Like who was the first man to drive the first T-bird ever distributed in San Francisco down the Great Highway racing the speedometer to 110 miles per hour? Why does everyone think blondes are stupid? And how many licks does it take to get to the center of a Tootsie Pop?

"We might have to do research and get some Tootsie Pops," said library manager Judy Flum with a laugh.

Then there were the philosophical questions: "If a tree falls in the forest and there is no one to hear it, does it make a sound?" and "Can deaf people hear themselves think?"

"If God can do anything, can he make a rock too heavy for himself to lift?" asked ninth-grader Danny Souza.

By the end of lunch Thursday, the students had four points on their side of the chalk board set up next to the table and the librarians had a stack of almost 200 questions. They have until April Fools' Day to find the answers.

Under the rules, a technical question will be considered answered if the librarians can tell the student how to find the answer.

"It's like the saying 'If you teach people to fish, it makes more sense them giving them fish,'" said project direct Stan Weisner.

Meaning-of-life questions, participants agreed, would be considered answered if the librarians can provide materials that say the question has conflicting theories or is unanswerable.

"We had quite a few (students) ask 'What came first — the chicken or the egg?'" said Gary Morrison, young-adult librarian for the San Lorenzo branch. "Hopefully, we'll come up with something that says there is no answer and we can Xerox the page."

Junior Rudy Felix was surprised to find that librarian Lael Takiguchi knew the answer to his question without having to resort to the 66 almanacs, atlases, encyclopedias and other reference books the librarians brought with them — everything from "The Book of Answers" to a fact book on the popular teen soap opera

> ❝ If God can do anything, can he make a rock too heavy for himself to lift?❞
>
> **Danny Souza**
> San Lorenzo ninth-grader, trying to stump a group of librarians

"Beverly Hills 90210."

"The Cincinnati Red Stockings," she said when the 17-year-old asked the name of the first baseball team. "Have you heard of the book 'If I Never Get Back?'" she quickly followed up. "It's an excellent book — a time-travel thing like 'Field of Dreams.'"

Felix said he regularly has to take his sister to the library but never checks books out himself.

"I look at 'Sports Illustrated,'" he said. But thanks to the visiting librarians, Felix said he's learned of a book he does want to check out: "Friday Night Lights," the story of a notorious high school football team.

"It's supposed to be one of the best football books ever," he said. "And I found out they have music and videos, and they said they have information on jobs."

Figure 18. Sample News Stories: General Public Relations

Libraries try rap, videos to woo teens

By Janet Weeks
Staff writer

Contra Costa librarians are hoping rap music and videos will lure teen-agers into the county's "uncool" libraries.

The county and Richmond are among nine public library systems participating in the federally funded Bay Area Youth at Risk Project. The project focuses on teen-agers, organizers say, because children and adults already use libraries.

"Teen-agers have fallen between the cracks and we are losing them as active consumers of information and good literature," says Stan Weisner, director of the project.

Image is part of the problem. Many teens see the library as a hangout for "intellectual nerds" only, says Stella Baker, community relations manager for Contra Costa County libraries.

A group of teens at Ygnacio Valley High School in Concord say the library is a good place for academic research, but it's sterile and dull.

"It's too quiet," says Michelle May, 14, a freshman. "I can't concentrate."

Wayne Wojcik, 17, a senior says: "No one really has a problem going there. If you have to research something, it's the place to go."

But he's turned off by library staffers who seem "402 years old."

Justin Krauss, 17, says he got a blank stare from a librarian when he asked for advice on science fiction paperbacks.

Similar stories were repeated by teens in focus groups organized by Youth at Risk, says Adelia Lines, director of the Richmond library system.

"There's a perception of the library as a kind of fuddy-duddy place," she says. "(Teens) don't see it as an 'in' place to be."

To make libraries more attractive to teens, Youth at Risk committees are creating a rap-style public service announcements for radio stations.

In Contra Costa, the Youth at Risk program will focus on the San Pablo branch with creation of a video resource center.

The library will collect educational videos about AIDS, violence, gangs and other issues for distribution to community groups that work with teens.

A demographic study shows San Pablo has the greatest need for improved communication between the library and teens. Also, the library staff shows the greatest interest in the program, Baker says.

The county also is printing 30,000 free "hip pocket" guides, pamphlets that will list phone numbers for a variety of teen resources. The guides will be ready next month.

In Richmond, the library system is getting involved by creating "Tutor Library Connection," or TLC. Once a week, librarians will work with youths involved in three free tutoring programs.

"We were concerned because of what had happened with our schools," Lines says. "School library programs are often the first to go in budget cuts."

Most librarians agree the best way to bring teens in is to give them their own room, where they can talk or eat without bothering other patrons. But most libraries are too small.

"One of the challenges of a public institution is trying to meet the needs of all its clients," Baker says. "It's a tough balancing act."

Youth at Risk is a pilot program funded by a $50,000 grant from the federal Library Services and Construction Act. If it's successful, similar programs will be organized throughout the state.

East Bay Edition

NEWS BRIEFS

■ REGION

Libraries' Plan to Lure Teenagers

San Francisco and East Bay librarians showcased plans to turn their reading rooms into "neutral, safe and relatively quiet" places for teenagers looking for ways to stay out of trouble.

The plans, developed under the federally financed Youth at Risk program, were developed after months of study by the nine library systems in San Francisco, Alameda and Contra Costa counties.

"Adolescents know that libraries exist, but they don't see them as interesting places to go," said Stan Weisner, director of the program.

"These plans will come up with programs that for the first time offer teens what they need. You can ask a librarian anything you want about sex, drugs and rock and roll, and you will find they have answers."

Weisner said the programs range from tutoring at Richmond libraries to a fine amnesty to encourage teenagers to return to libraries in San Francisco.

The programs include links with schools and other agencies to keep Oakland teenagers from dropping out and enlisting Berkeley youths in a "Youth Outreach Corps."

88

Librarians hip to teen needs

Books are loaned but advice is free

By Don Martinez
OF THE EXAMINER STAFF

OAKLAND — Librarians from throughout the Bay Area have outlined a strategy to make their traditionally nerdy emporiums of knowledge more hip in efforts to attract troubled teen-agers.

Officials from libraries in San Francisco, Alameda and Contra Costa counties gathered at Oakland's main branch Monday to kick off the Bay Area Youth at Risk Project.

Funded by a $150,000 federal grant, the program is designed to bring youngsters from 12 to 19 back into the public library system.

"Libraries have traditionally done a good job serving children and adults, but most teen-agers have sort of slipped through our system," said Dr. Stan Weisner, director of the yearlong pilot program in nine library districts.

"We want to tell these kids that they can ask their librarian anything about sex, drugs and rock 'n' roll and find the answer," Weisner said.

State Librarian Gary Strong, on hand to help launch the regional program, said, "Youngsters don't realize that libraries are a neutral meeting ground in which people can obtain information on issues important to them."

Neel Parikh, chief of San Francisco's 26 branch libraries, said one of her primary targets are teen-agers in the Hunters Point-Bayview District.

"We're setting up a committee of youngsters and community leaders from that community to determine what it is youngsters want from their branch library," Parikh said.

Oakland Library Director Martin Gomez said a special homework tutoring program will begin next month at the East Oakland branch at Foothill Boulevard and East 14th Street.

"We're going to have tutors on hand in the hours after school to help teens with their homework and to show them how to do their own research and access resource material they need for their studies," Gomez said.

Library drive hopes to make books part of teenagers' lives

■ *Advocates emphasize topics with relevence to at-risk kids.*

By Cheryl Bealer
The Montclarion

AIDS, premarital sex and drugs are a few of the topics a group of library advocates are hoping will lure teenagers back to the shelves and away from dropping out of school.

"Libraries have traditionally not been accessible to at-risk kids," said Stan Weisner, head of the Bay Area Youth at Risk Project, who appeared at Oakland's Main Library this week to kick off the drive.

"But libraries are actually the perfect environment because (youths) are not being graded or tested and the information isn't being filtered to them through their parents or family. They can get straight information about anything they want."

The program will consist of different teen-targeted activities at nine Bay Area libraries, surveyed by The Youth at Risk group several months ago. The two-year, $600,000 program is funded with federal and state grants and donations.

Oakland's Martin Luther King branch library will receive $6,000 to start an afterschool homework and tutoring center this November.

In addition, program leaders plan to teach teens how to find information in the library and introduce them to new facets of libraries, such as compact disc collections, videotapes and computers.

The center will focus on combatting the city's 31 percent high school drop-out rate, which is perceived to be one of the worst problems facing Oakland, according to the survey.

The dropout rate — 11 percent higher than the statewide average — was ranked third only to family problems and drugs and alcohol as the most serious problems cited by community leaders, according to project leaders.

Weisner, a Montclair resident, said Youth At Risk leaders hope to expand the afterschool program to other branch libraries in the future.

"Teens all over Oakland need to be better served by public libraries, like the one my kids use in Montclair ... this is an important first step for Oakland's library system." ■

Page 88, left: September 30, 1991 / West County Times; right: October 1,1991 / San Francisco Chronicle

This page, above: October 1,1991 / San Francisco Examiner; below: October 4, 1991 / The Montclarion

89

Getting the Word Out About Teen Library Services

Background

You have been asked to disseminate information to the teen population and the general public about library services for teens in your community.

Tasks

■ **Create a message and a means to get the word out to youth and the community at large about YA services in your library.**

1. Identify ten ways (e.g., TV, radio, billboards, student newspapers, flyers on community billboards, etc.) that you could try to reach teens in your community.

2. Draft a statement (a press release or program flyer) that announces a new (or ongoing) teen library program or service at your branch. Use words and images that will create enthusiasm as well as convey information in a concise manner about your upcoming event.

■ **Develop a strategy for convening a special teen event and getting positive press coverage from local media.**

1. What is the essential point or message you hope to get out to the public?

2. Develop an outline for a packet of materials for the press and draft a brief "sound bite" to use if a reporter were to ask you to say something about library services for teens in twenty seconds or less.

CHAPTER X.   # Advocacy for Children and Youth: A Key Role for Librarians

"We must build a corps of advocates if tomorrow's library system is to meet the challenges we recognize today."

> —delegate to the White House Conference on Library and Information Services, quoted in the February 3, 1992 edition of *Library Hotline* (Vol. XXI, No. 25)

Effective advocacy requires the development of a consistent strategy to speak out on behalf of a particular group or issue. Children's and YA librarians need to find ways to voice the concerns of the young people they serve both within the library system and the community at large. This will involve competing for resources internally as well as in the budget and legislative arena at the local, state and national levels. The delivery of services to at-risk children and youth give public libraries a powerful message in their role as advocates.

At the same time that librarians advocate for youth — which, in this book, have been defined as teens age twelve to eighteen — it makes sense to advocate for children. The interests of the two groups are closely linked, and advocacy is an important area in which to recognize this connection. The earlier that attention is given to children and youth at risk, the more effectively their problems can be addressed. This chapter, then, addresses advocacy for both children and youth.

WHY advocate for children and youth services

- To combat the deteriorating status of our youth, as evidenced by high poverty rates, high teen pregnancy rates, falling school budgets, and falling scholastic test scores
- To highlight innovative and effective services for children and youth
- To gain political support for public libraries and their delivery of services to at-risk youth

WHAT constitutes advocacy for children and youth services

Child advocacy is growing as a movement in the United States. Most public opinion polls show the growing awareness in the United States of the deteriorating status of our children and youth. Over forty states now have statewide child advocacy organizations. A prototype in California is the group California Now. There are also many local child advocacy groups who monitor the status of youth in each city or county. Nationally, the Children's Defense Fund in Washington, D.C. and the Association of Child Advocates (a membership group of state organizations) have served as primary voices for the needs of children.

In addition to these more general child advocacy organizations, there are a large number of child advocates in the fields of child welfare, mental health, pediatrics, education, etc. who speak out about special needs of children and youth. Children's and young adult librarians have also organized to improve the level of services. For example, there is the Children's and Young Adult Services Section of the California Library Association. At the national level, there is the Association for Library Service to Children. For teen services, there is the Young Adult Library Services Association of the American Library Association.

A strong advocacy voice for at-risk youth is needed among librarians at all levels. At the local level, YA librarians need to be involved in efforts to coordinate services within the library and in the community. At the state and federal level, YA librarians need to be involved in the development of legislation which will affect the funding levels of services for youth. Currently, "only eleven percent of the nation's public libraries have the services of a young adult librarian" (National Center for Education Statistics, 1988, p.1). The White House Conference on Library and Information Services is recommending that services to at-risk youth become one of the highest legislative priorities in the years ahead.

HOW to be an advocate for children and youth

There are at least three types of child/youth advocacy:
- administrative — making sure current policies and programs for children and youth are being implemented in their best interests
- judicial — ensuring that the laws affecting the quality of life for children and youth are being adequately interpreted and enforced
- legislative — working to develop legislation at all levels of government that improve the quality of life for children and youth

Public librarians can become active in a number of ways both within the library community and in collaboration with other professional and citizen groups to improve the status of children and youth at the local, regional, or national level. Some suggestions for becoming active are listed below:

How-to Checklist: Advocacy for Youth

☐ Join a local or regional YA librarians' association.

☐ Join a more general child/youth advocacy organization and become involved in their activities (publicity, lobbying, organizing, etc.).

☐ Organize staff in your library who are interested in teens and advocate for YA services on their behalf within the library system and in the community (attend special hearings and neighborhood meetings, write letters to the editor, etc.).

☐ Become informed about the needs of teens in your community and speak out on their behalf as a public librarian concerned about youth issues. This can be especially useful at the local level when city and county budget decisions are being made.

☐ Find out about current or pending state and/or federal legislation expanding services for at-risk youth and write letters in favor of bills which support children and youth.

Advocacy in the YAR Project

In each of the nine YAR Project communities, there has been an increased awareness among other child and youth-serving organizations of the role that librarians can play with at-risk youth. In all three counties served by BALIS libraries, YAR Project Steering Committee members got involved in county coordinating councils working on similar issues. Local media coverage of a variety of YAR Project programs has raised the profile of youth at risk issues and the library's role in addressing those needs.

At the opening session of one of the YAR Project trainings, the president of the major statewide child advocacy organization in California (Children Now) received a rousing reception as keynote speaker. In San Francisco, a local advocacy organization (Coleman Advocates for Children and Youth) lobbied against cuts in library services (see sample of petition to mayor's office in Figure 19).

"We've lost a generation, and I think public libraries are aware of that. Libraries are not going to stamp out teen-age pregnancy, but there are areas where they have some strengths, where they can help."

— BALIS YAR Project administrator

At the national level, the BALIS YAR Project was the subject of a presentation at the 1992 American Library Association Conference. At the state level, the youth at risk agenda was a top priority of the California Library Services Board and has been the subject of major workshop presentations at two consecutive California Library Association conferences. The California State Library is also now listed on the widely distributed "Guide to State Agencies Serving Children" published each year. One of the expected outcomes of the YAR Project is the development of statewide legislation which will focus attention on the plight of youth at risk.

Figure 19. Sample Petition for Advocacy

 **Dear Mayor Jordan,**

We, the undersigned, <u>protest any further cuts in the library budget</u>. We believe our community library services are one of the best dollar values in city services and <u>we support the use of our tax dollars for increasing these services</u>. Libraries provide invaluable, cost-effective programs to our city's children and must be maintained to implement the intent of Proposition J, The Children's Amendment.

Name _____

Address_____

_____

Comments: _____

Name _____

Address_____

_____

Comments: _____

Name _____

Address _____

_____

Comments: _____

We encourage you to copy and circulate this petition. Thanks!

A Petition From
San Francisco Voters

stamp

Mayor Frank Jordan
Room 200, City Hall
San Francisco, California 94102

 OUR <u>CHILDREN</u>
NEED LIBRARIES!

In the past five years public access to our libraries has been cut 24%. The Mayor has now proposed additional reductions of 10%, which will severely cripple our libraries, <u>leaving most open only two days a week and no Saturdays</u>. Libraries, in many neighborhoods, are the most frequented place to go after school and the only community resource for children. They are essential to the literacy, safety, school performance and cultural enrichment of our young people. Proposition J mandates increased library services for children - how can children's needs be met if the hours and resources of our community-based libraries are not maintained? Send a clear message to Mayor Jordan that library cuts are unacceptable to our children.

<u>DRAW THE LINE NOW - STOP THE CUTS!</u>

Advocacy for Children and Youth

Background

A recent report is released on the status of children and youth in your county. School test scores are dropping, teen pregnancy and STD rates are soaring, child abuse and neglect reports are increasing. It has been suggested that a community meeting should be convened to respond to the worsening conditions of teens.

Tasks

■ Identify three issues and advocacy strategies that would highlight the plight of at-risk youth in your community.

■ What other child/youth advocacy groups might you contact and begin to work with? What common issues would you address?

Selected Bibliography

Young Adult Services (General)

American Library Association. *Look, Listen, Explain: Developing Community Library Services for Young Adults.* Chicago: American Library Association, 1975.

Boegen, Anne, ed. *Young Adult Services Manual.* Tallahassee: Florida State Library, 1986.

Jones, Patrick. *Connecting Young Adults and Libraries: A How-To-Do-It-Manual.* New York: Neal-Schuman Publishers, 1992.

LiBretto, Ellen V. *New Directions for Young Adult Services.* New York: R.R. Bowker Company, 1983.

National Center for Education Statistics. *Services and Resources for Young Adults in Public Libraries.* Washington: U.S. Department of Education, Office of Educational Research and Improvement (CS 88-418), 1988.

New Jersey State Library. *Guidelines for Young Adult Services in Public Libraries of New Jersey.* Trenton: New Jersey State Department of Education, 1987.

Washington Library Association. *Advocating Access: Developing Community Library Services for Children and Young Adults in Washington State.* Bellevue: Washington Library Association, Young Adult Services Division, 1989.

Youth at Risk (General)

Dryfoos, Joy. *Adolescents-at-Risk: Prevalence and Prevention.* New York: Oxford University Press, 1990.

Irwin, Charles. "The Theoretical Concept of At-risk Adolescents." *Adolescent Medicine* 1 (February 1990): 1-13.

Kirst, Michael. *Conditions of Children in California.* Berkeley: Policy Analysis for California Education (PACE), School of Education, University of California at Berkeley, 1989.

Miller, Frances, ed. *Under 18 and Unhappy at Home?* Livermore, California: Livermore Public Library, 1992.

Rockefeller, Jay D. *Beyond Rhetoric: A New Agenda For Children and Families.* Washington: National Commission on Children, 1990.

Wells, Shirley E. *At-Risk Youth: Identification, Programs and Recommendations.* Englewood, Colorado: Teacher Ideas Press, 1990.

Needs Assessment	Neuber, Keith A. *Needs Assessment: A Model for Community Planning*. Beverly Hills: Sage Publications, 1980.
	Herman, Joan. *Evaluator's Handbook*. New York: Sage Publications, 1987.
	Partnerships for Change. *Community-based Needs Assessment*. Sacramento: California State Library, 1990.
Community Involvement	Bodart, Joni. *Booktalk! Booktalking and School Visiting for Young Adult Audiences*. Bronx: H.W. Wilson, 1980.
	Brilz, Linda. "The Quest for the Elusive YA (You've Got to Have a Grabber That Will Bring Them In)." *School Library Journal* 35 (December 1988): 46.
	Chang, Hedy Nai-Lin, et al. *Fighting Fragmentation: Collaborative Efforts to Serve Children and Families in California's Counties*. Berkeley: California Tomorrow and The Children and Youth Policy Project, University of California at Berkeley, 1991.
	Sasges, Judy and Mary Moore. "Juvenile Hall Library Service on a Part-time Basis." *Voice of Youth Advocates* (June 1982): 12-16.
Advisory Committees	Ponzini, Suzanne M. and Sheldon L. Tarakan. "Input and Output: The Functioning of a Youth Advisory Council." *The Bookmark* 43, No. III (Spring 1985): 130-133.
	Truccillo, Diane. "A Young Adult Advisory Council Can Work For You." *Emergency Librarian* (May-June 1986): 15-16.
Plan Development	Jones, Patrick. "Know Your P's and Q's: A Planning Process for Young Adult Programs." *Journal of Youth Services in Libraries* 2 (Fall 1988): 95-100.
	Public Library Development Project. *Planning and Role Setting for Public Libraries*. Chicago: American Library Association, 1987.
	Public Library Association. *Planning for Children's Services in Public Libraries*. Chicago: Public Library Association, 1985.
Proposal Writing	Cory, Emmett. *Grants for Libraries: A Guide to Public and Private Funding Programs and Proposal Writing Techniques*. Littleton, Colorado: Libraries Unlimited, 1986.
	Kiritz, Norton J. and Jerry Mundel. *Program Planning and Proposal Writing*. Los Angeles: The Grantsmanship Center, 1988.

Evaluation

Berk, Richard A. and Peter H. Rossi. *Thinking about Program Evaluation.* Newbury Park, California: Sage, 1990.

Chelton, Mary K. "Developmentally-based Performance Measures for Young Adults." *Top of the News* (Fall 1984): 39-52.

Harder, Paul. *Serving Youth at Risk: An Evaluation of the Bay Area Library and Information System Projects, 1991-1992.* San Francisco: Harder+Kibbe Research and Consulting, August 11, 1992.

Public Library Development Project. *Output Measures for Public Libraries.* Chicago: American Library Association, 1987.

Walter, Virginia A. *Output Measures for Public Library Service to Children.* Chicago: American Library Association, 1992.

Multicultural/ Multiethnic Services

Allen, Adela Artola, ed. "Library Services for Hispanic Young Adults." *Library Trends* 37, No. 1 (Summer 1988): 80-105.

California Tomorrow. *Embracing Diversity: Teachers' Voices from California Classrooms.* California Tommorrow, 1990.

Liestman, Daniel. *Library Users Whose Second Language is English: A Bibliography of Sources, 1964-1989.* New Brunswick, New Jersey: Rutgers State University, 1989.

Liu, Grace F. *Promoting Library Awareness in Ethnic Communities.* Santa Clara, California: South Bay Cooperative Library System, 1985.

Payne, Judith. *Public Libraries Face California's Ethnic and Racial Diversity.* Santa Monica: Rand Corporation, 1988.

Scarborough, Katharine T.A. *Developing Library Collections for California's Emerging Majority: A Manual of Resources for Ethnic Collection Development.* Oakland: Bay Area Library and Information System, 1990.

Willet, Holly. "The Changing Demographics of Children's Services." *Journal of Youth Services in Libraries* 2, No. 1 (Fall 1988): 40-50.

Training

Lipow, Anne and Deborah Carver. *Staff Development: A Practical Guide.* Chicago: American Library Association, 1992.

Waddle, Linda. *Cheap CE: Providing Continuing Education with Limited Resources, A Practical Guide.* Chicago: Education Committee, Young Adult Services Division, American Library Association, 1981.

Publicity and Public Relations

Dratch-Kovler, Carol. "Young Adult Services' Public Relations and Promotion." *The Bookmark* 43 (Spring 1985): 107-110.

Rogers, Jo Ann, ed. *Libraries and Young Adults: Media Services and Librarianship.* Littleton, Colorado: Libraries Unlimited, 1979.

Advocacy

Minudri, Regina. "How to Win Friends and Influence Administrators." *School Library Journal* (January 1976): 33.

Sunley, Robert. *Advocating Today: A Human Services Practitioner's Handbook.* New York: Family Service Association, 1983.

Wilson, Evie. "The Librarian as Advocate for Youth." In *Reaching Young People Through Media*, edited by Nancy Bach Pillon, 155-180. Littleton, Colorado: Libraries Unlimited, 1983.

N.B. Consult *Journal of Youth Services in Libraries*, the official journal of the Association for Library Service to Children and the Young Adult Library Services Association of the American Library Association.

Appendices

Youth at Risk Project Timeline

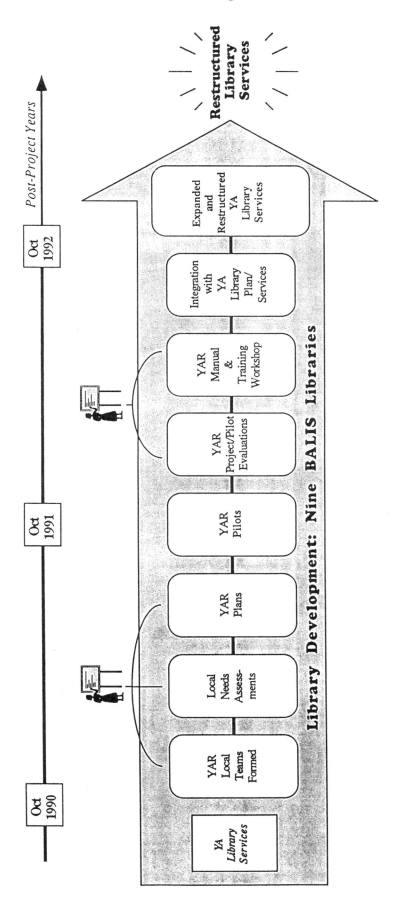

Restructured Library Services

Post-Project Years

Oct 1992

Oct 1991

Oct 1990

Library Development: Nine BALIS Libraries

Expanded and Restructured YA Library Services

Integration with YA Library Plan/Services

YAR Manual & Training Workshop

YAR Project/Pilot Evaluations

YAR Pilots

YAR Plans

Local Needs Assessments

YAR Local Teams Formed

YA Library Services

Sample Youth at Risk Team Roster

BAY AREA YOUTH AT RISK PROJECT
LOCAL YAR TEAM ROSTER
HAYWARD PUBLIC LIBRARY

Library Representatives

Cindy Carhart	Children's Librarian
Mary Dlugosz	Young Adult Librarian
Sherry Kumler (Committee Chair)	Youth Services Manager

Community Representatives

Art Elliot	Hayward Police Department
Jennifer Johnson	Youth Member
Tak Kato	Juvenile Court
Alison Lewis	Eden Youth Center
David Mattingly	Hayward Unified School District
Sherril Spellman	Winton Junior High School (Librarian)

APPENDIX C. **Consultant Contract Sample**

BAY AREA LIBRARY AND INFORMATION SYSTEM

STANDARD AGREEMENT

THIS AGREEMENT, made and entered into this ___16th___ day of _April___,
19__, by and between the Bay Area Library and Information System, State of
California, hereinafter called the System, and _Marilyn Smulyan_____
_____ hereinafter called the Contractor.

WITNESSETH: That the Contractor for and in consideration of the covenants,
conditions, agreements, and stipulations of the System hereinafter expressed,
does hereby agree to furnish to the System services and materials, as follows,
and/or as described on exhibits attached to and incorporated herein.

(Set forth: 1) Service to be rendered by Contract; 2) Program receiving service;
3) Contractor's qualifications; 4) Additional provisions incorporated.)

Design and implement study of youth at risk in San Francisco
which will include interviews (10-15 face-to-face; 30-40
telephone) with key informants, and 3-4 focus groups.

Complete written needs assessment and draft recommendations
on Young Adult library services in 30-40 page report that
includes findings from interviews and focus groups and
incorporates data from provider survey and demographic
data.

Present draft report to San Francisco Youth-At-Risk team
and prepare final report by July 31, 1991.

Page 1 of 4

520 THIRD STREET • SUITE 202 • OAKLAND • CA 94607-3520
BAY AREA LIBRARY AND INFORMATION SYSTEM   SYSTEM OFFICE: 415/839-6001; REFERENCE CENTER: 415/839-5447
FAX: 415/834-5193

MEMBER LIBRARIES: ALAMEDA FREE LIBRARY (CITY); ALAMEDA COUNTY LIBRARY; BERKELEY PUBLIC LIBRARY; CONTRA COSTA COUNTY LIBRARY;
HAYWARD PUBLIC LIBRARY; LIVERMORE PUBLIC LIBRARY; OAKLAND PUBLIC LIBRARY; RICHMOND PUBLIC LIBRARY; SAN FRANCISCO PUBLIC LIBRARY.

CONTRACT PERIOD will be from _____ through _____.

COMPENSATION: System agrees to pay Contractor for services performed hereunder at the rate of $_____ per _____and/or in accordance with the following payment schedule:

The total amount paid by System to Contractor under this agreement shall not exceed the sum of $_____.

ADDITIONAL PROVISIONS set forth on the reverse hereof constitute a part of this agreement.

IN WITNESS WHEREOF, the parties hereto have executed this agreement as of the date and year first above written.

BAY AREA LIBRARY AND INFORMATION SYSTEM   CONTRACTOR

By _____   _____
    Chairperson, Administrative Council
                                            By _____

                                            _____
                                                        (Title)

                                            _____

                                            _____
                                                        (Address)

BALIS-115 6/82
L2:StdAgreemt

Page 2 of 4

106

ADDITIONAL PROVISIONS - BALIS STANDARD AGREEMENT

1. Contractor agrees that it is an independent Contractor and that its officers and employees do not become employees of the System nor are they entitled to any employee benefits as System Employees as a result of the execution of this agreement.

2. Contractor shall indemnify System, its officers and employees against liability for injury or damage caused by any negligent act or omission of any of its employees or volunteers or agents in the performance of this agreement and shall hold System harmless from any loss occasioned as a result of the performance of this contract by Contractor. The Contractor shall provide necessary Workman's Compensation insurance at Contractor's own cost and expense.

3. No officer, member or employee of System and no member of their governing bodies shall have any pecuniary interest, direct or indirect, in this agreement or the proceeds thereof. No employee of Contractor nor any member of an employee's family shall serve on a System board, committee or hold any such position which either by rule, practice or action nominates, recommends, supervises Contractor's operations or authorizes funding to Contractor.

4. Contractor may not assign or transfer this agreement, any interest therein or claim thereunder without the prior written approval of System.

5. Payment to Contractor will be made only upon presentation of a proper claim by Contractor subject to approval of the System Auditor-Controller.

6. System shall have access to Contractor's financial records for purposes of audit. Such records shall be complete and available for audit 90 days after final payment hereunder and shall be retained and available for audit purposes for five years after final payment hereunder.

7. System may terminate this agreement at any time by giving Contractor a thirty (30) day written notice of such sooner termination and may be terminated at any time without notice upon a material breach of the terms of this agreement by Contractor. Contractor may terminate this agreement at any time by giving System a thirty (30) day written notice of such sooner termination.

8. Time is of the essence in each and all the provisions of this agreement.

9. No alteration or variation of the terms of this agreement shall be valid unless made in writing and signed by the parties hereto.

Page 3 of 4

10. Contractor shall not be allowed or paid travel expenses unless set forth in this agreement.

11. Contractor assures that it will comply with Title VI of the Civil Rights Act of 1964 and that no person shall, on the grounds of race, creed, color, sex or national origin be excluded from participation in, be denied the benefits of, or be otherwise subjected to discrimination under this agreement.

12. System shall have a royalty-free, non-exclusive, and irrevocable license to reproduce, publish, use, and to authorize others to do so, all original computer programs, writing, sound recordings, pictorial reproductions, drawings and other works of similar nature produced in the course of or under this agreement; and Contractor shall not publish any such material without prior written consent of System.

13. Contractor agrees that determinations of rights to inventions made in the course of or under this agreement shall be made by System, and that System shall acquire an irrevocable, non-exclusive, and royalty-free license to practice and use, and let any public agency practice and use, any such invention.

BALIS-115 6/82
L2:StdAgreemt

Page 4 of 4

Youth Survey and Youth Services
Provider Mailed Questionnaires

WIN A DOOR PRIZE BY FILLING OUT THIS SURVEY
AND RETURNING TO THE LIBRARY TABLE!

YOUTH QUESTIONNAIRE
FOR
BERKELEY CITY WIDE YOUTH FORUM
March 27, 1991

Your Name:_____

The Berkeley Young Adult librarians would like to find out what you want from the public library. Please answer the questions below. Your participation is voluntary and your answers will be kept confidential.

1. What <u>kinds of information</u> do you feel the public libraries in Berkeley should have available for youth?

2. What <u>afterschool activities and programs</u> do you feel the public libraries in Berkeley should have available to youth?

3. How often do you use a public library?

    ____ at least once a week   ____ at least once a year
    ____ at least once a month   ____ almost never

4. If you currently use the library, what do you use it for? (check one or more).

    ____ taking out books/videos/tapes/records/magazines for personal use
    ____ using the equipment (copy machine, typewriter, etc.)
    ____ getting reference materials for school projects
    ____ doing your homework or completing school assignment
    ____ meeting and talking with your friends
    ____ attending a special program for youth
    ____ other_____   (over)

5. What would make the library easier for you to use? (check three).

    ____ more staff to help you find things
    ____ computer catalogue instruction
    ____ more comfortable chairs/tables
    ____ greater selection of books/materials for youth
    ____ youth programs on special topics (e.g. car repair, health, careers, etc.)
    ____ other_____

6. If a youth advisory committee were available at your library, would you participate?

__ Yes   __ No

7. What is the ONE thing the library could do to make you want to use it more often?

8. What do you think are the most important issues facing Berkeley teenagers today? (check three).

____ lack of summer jobs	____ sexually transmitted diseases
____ poor schools	____ AIDS
____ family problems	____ gang violence
____ lack of recreation programs	____ racial discrimination
____ drug and alchohol abuse	____ other_____

Information about yourself:

School:_____   Grade:_____

Ethnic Background:_____   Gender: Male____ Female___

Thank you for your participation in the survey!!!
Make sure you hand in the completed survey at the library for you chance at a door prize!

Alameda
Free Library

20-May-91

Thank you for agreeing to administer the library's Youth Questionnaire. Enclosed are   questionnaires and a copy of the Focus Group questions.

The Task Force had some suggestions that may make the Focus Groups run more smoothly for you as the discussion leader.

> ** Use an overhead projector to take notes. Write on a transparency (single sheets). These sheets can be xeroxed directly.

> ** Appoint a recorder for the group (depending on the age level) if you don't have an overhead projector. It is often difficult to remember all the details of the discussion and notes don't have to be transcribed from the chalkboard.

> ** Do use the focus group questions as a GUIDE. Try to address those questions, but don't force a discussion just to follow them. All suggestions, comments and observations from these discussions will be useful and are most welcome!

Please try to keep class sets of the questionnaires together, i.e. ESL, Leadership, grade levels etc. You may want to attach the focus group notes to each set of questions if a focus group was conducted.

We would like to receive the questionnaires back during the week of June 3rd. This will give us a little time to look at the responses before our June 10th meeting. Please feel free to call me if you need more questionnaires or have any problems or questions about the project.

Thanks again for all your valuable help. We couldn't do this project without you!

Sincerely,

Jane Chisaki
Supervising Librarian
Children's Services

YOUTH QUESTIONNAIRE
FOR
ALAMEDA FREE LIBRARY
May 1991

Your Name (optional):_____

The Alameda Free Library would like to find out what you want from the public library. Please answer the questions below. Your participation is voluntary and your answers will be kept confidential.

1.   How often do you use a public library?

_____ at least once a week   _____ at least once a year
_____ at least once a month   _____ almost never   _____ never

2.   Do you know where any of the public libraries are in Alameda?

_____ Yes   _____ No

Do you have a library card?

_____ Yes   _____ No

(Check one   3.   If you currently use the library, what do you use it for?
or more.)

_____ taking out books/videos/tapes/records/magazines for personal use
_____ using the equipment (copy machine, reader/printer)
_____ getting reference materials for school projects
_____ doing your homework or completing school assignments
_____ meeting and talking with your friends
_____ attending a special program for youth
_____ other _____

(Check   4.   What would make the library easier for you to use?
three.)

_____ more open hours - times: _____
_____ more staff to help you find things
_____ computer catalog instruction
_____ more comfortable chairs/tables
_____ greater selection of books/materials for youth
_____ youth programs on special topics (e.g. car repair, health, careers, etc.)
_____ signs (directional/informational)
_____ other _____

(OVER)

112

5. If a youth advisory committee were available at your public library, would you participate?

    _____ Yes _____ No

    If yes, please give name and address: _____
    _____
    _____

6. What is the ONE thing the library could do to make you want to use it more often?

7. What do you think are the most important issues facing Alameda teenagers today?

    _____ lack of summer jobs   _____ AIDS
    _____ not doing well in school   _____ gang violence
    _____ family problems   _____ understanding people from different
    _____ lack of recreation programs   cultures
    _____ drug and alcohol abuse   _____ handling problems with other
    _____ peer pressure   students
    _____ no one to talk to   _____ teen pregnancy
    _____ sexually transmitted diseases   _____ other _____

    (Indicate with a * the ones that are most important to you.)

8. Where do you go to get information you need to make decisions about problems you face:
    _____ the library   _____ coaches/recreation leaders
    _____ books, magazines, TV   _____ churches
    _____ school (teachers/counselors)   _____ doctors
    _____ friends   _____ special teen programs
    _____ parents/relatives   _____ other _____

9. What kinds of information do you feel the public libraries in Alameda should have available for youth?

10. What after school activities and programs do you feel the public libraries in Alameda should have available to youth?

Information about yourself:

School:_____   Grade:_____

Ethnic Background: ___White ___ Black   Male ___ Female ___
                    ___ Asian or Pacific Islander
                    ___ Hispanic
                    ___ American Indian or Alaskan Native

Language(s) Spoken at Home:_____

_____

THANK YOU FOR YOUR PARTICIPATION IN THE SURVEY!!!

BAY AREA YOUTH-AT-RISK PROJECT
FUNDED BY THE CALIFORNIA STATE LIBRARY
THROUGH THE LIBRARY SERVICES AND
CONSTRUCTION ACT

Bay Area Youth at Risk Project

520 Third Street • Suite 202 • Oakland, CA 94607-3520
Telephone: 415/839-4593 • FAX: 415/834-5193

May 10, 1991

Dear Youth Service Provider:

  The Bay Area Youth-at-Risk Project of the Bay Area Library and Information System is working with public libraries throughout the Bay Area to develop and expand programs for at-risk youth ages 12-18.

  The first phase of the project is to survey directors and staff of local youth-serving agencies about the needs of at-risk youth in their communities. Data from the survey will provide the foundation for focus groups of youth and others to develop ideas for local public library programs for at-risk youth.

  Public libraries can play an important role in the lives of teenagers if programs can be created that complement the existing network of youth services. Information and knowledge can be a source of empowerment for youth of all ages.

  We hope that you will participate in this project by taking about 15 minutes to respond to the enclosed survey on the needs of at-risk youth in your community or directing it to the person on your staff most knowledgeable about high-risk youth.

  We would like the questionnaire returned to us in the enclosed stamped self-addressed envelope by May 28.

  Thank you very much for your assistance.

Sincerely,

Stan Weisner

Stan Weisner
Project Director

Enclosures

YOUTH SERVICES PROVIDER QUESTIONNAIRE
LIBRARY SERVICES FOR YOUTH

BAY AREA YOUTH-AT-RISK PROJECT
FUNDED BY THE CALIFORNIA STATE LIBRARY
THROUGH THE LIBRARY SERVICES AND
CONSTRUCTION ACT

This brief questionnaire is aimed at helping public libraries in your community shape programs for at-risk youth ages 12-18. Please answer the following questions based on your experience and knowledge of youth issues in your community.

Thank you very much for your help.

Your Name _____

Agency _____

Phone Number _____

Please circle the number next to the appropriate answer.

1. Primary youth population served by your agency:

    1   12-14 years   2   15-18 years

2. Program focus (*circle all that apply*):

    1 Health   6 Youth advocacy and planning
    2 Education and tutoring   7 Substance abuse
    3 Recreation   8 Mental health
    4 Youth employment/job training 9 Youth development and leadership
    5 Child welfare   10 Other: _____

3. What specific geographic area do you serve: _____

4. In your opinion, what are the <u>three</u> most serious problems or risks teenagers face in your community in the 1990's? (*Please rank order the top <u>three</u> problems for each age group, with 1 = the most serious problem, 2 = second most serious problem, 3 = third most serious problem*)

	Younger teens (12-14 years)	Older teens (15-18 years)
1 Drugs/Alcohol		
2 Involvement in crime		
3 Teenage pregnancy		
4 Dropping out of school		
5 Lack of employment opportunities		
6 Literary below grade level		
7 STDs/AIDS		
8 Family problems		
9 Lack of recreation programs		
10 Racial discrimination		
11 Other:		

5. If you had to choose, which special group of youth in your community stands out as being most underserved? (*Circle all appropriate numbers to define one group.*)

1 Boys
   1a   12-14
   1b   15-18
   1c   both

2 Girls

   2a   12-14
   2b   15-18
   2c   both

3 Both sexes and all ages

4 Ethnic groups
   4a   Hispanics
   4b   Whites
   4c   African-Americans
   4d   Asians
   4e   Other: _____

5 Immigrant/refugee populations
   5a   Southeast Asians
   5b   Central Americans
   5c   Other: _____

6 Other: _____
   _____

6. Below is a list of needs of youth. In your opinion, what are the three most serious needs that are currently not adequately met in your community? (*Please circle and rank order the top three needs with 1 indicating the most serious need, 2 the second most serious and 3 the third most serious need.*)

1	Summer jobs	9	Recreation
2	Tutoring	10	Career counseling/job training
3	Alcohol/drug education	11	Alcohol/drug treatment
4	Child welfare/protection	12	Sex education
5	Other health education	13	Cultural awareness
6	Programs for gay/lesbian youth	14	Legal advice
7	Remedial education	15	Mentoring
8	Information and referral	16	Family stability
17	Other: _____		

_____

7. Below is a list of programs some public libraries offer youth. (*Please circle and rank order the three programs you think would have the most impact on the subgroup of youth you indicated above as most underserved, with 1 indicating the program with the most impact, etc.*) Add any others you think may be effective.

1	Information/referral	6	Summer job information
2	Community outreach (school visits, community agencies, etc.)	7	Support groups/counseling
		8	Health education/information
3	Special events programs (job fairs, speakers, concerts)	9	Tutoring/tutoring referral
		10	Bookmobile
4	Homework help	11	Other: _____
5	Ethnic literature development		

_____

8. Should public library services for young adults be offered outside of existing library facilities?

1	Yes	2	No

9. If Yes, where should these services be? (Please circle three places you feel library services would be most effective/reach the most needy teens.)

1	Shopping malls	6	School sites
2	Recreation centers	7	Juvenile hall
3	Neighborhood centers	8	Public housing sites
4	Restaurants (Burger King, etc.)	9	Drug/alcohol treatment programs
5	Arcades/Amusement parks	10	Other: _____

10. Please tell us a little about yourself:

Your current job title: _____

Your age

    1 20-29   2 30-39   3 over 40

Your ethnicity

    1 African-American 2 White   3 Hispanic   4 Asian

    5 Other: _____

How long have you worked with youth?

    1 less than 1 year   2 1-4 years   3 5 + years

How long have you worked in this community?

    1 less than 1 year   2 1-4 years   3 5 + years

11. Would you be interested in participating in a follow-up meeting to discuss the needs of youth and the role that public libraries might play in creatively meeting those needs?

            YES ___   NO ____

Do you know of others who might be interested in such a meeting? (*Please list their names, agencies and phone numbers.*)

Please use this space for any other comments:

Thank you for completing this questionnaire. Please return it in the enclosed stamped addressed envelope <u>no later than May 28</u> to:

**Bay Area Youth-at-Risk Project, c/o CAL Research,
183 Broadway, Richmond, CA 94804.**

Sample Youth Services Provider Interview Questions

Hello, my name is _____. I am calling from the Youth at Risk Project which is sponsored by the local library system. This project is working with public libraries in _____ to develop recommendations for improving library services for high-risk youth between the ages of twelve and eighteen.

As an integral part of exploring how to expand and redefine traditional library roles for youth services, we are interested in talking to service providers such as yourself who are working with youth on a daily basis.

The interview should only take about twenty minutes and your comments will be kept confidential.

First, I'd like to ask you a few questions about your agency and its services.

1. What services do you provide to youth?

2. What is the predominant ethnicity of the youth served by your agency?

3. Are the youth served by your agency mostly male or female?

4. What is the age range of the youth served by your agency?

5. Are the youth served by your agency generally from a specific district or geographical area? Which?

Now I have a few questions about the specific needs of the youth served by your agency.

6. What are the major problems or issues facing the youth served by your agency? List the top three.

Drugs/alcohol	Crime involvement	Teen pregnancy
School drop-outs	Unemployment	Literacy level
STDs/AIDS	Family problems	Lack of rec programs
Discrimination	Gang involvement	Other

7. Are there any other specific problems?

8. Which group of youth in your community stands out as being the most underserved?

9. Where are the greatest gaps in services for youth in your community?

10. What are the three most urgent needs of youth in your community?

The remaining questions address the ways in which your local library might be used as a resource for youth at risk.

11. What services can public libraries provide to address youth problems and needs?

12. How can the public library better meet the multicultural/multilingual needs of youth in your community?

13. How can the library serve the youth who are also served by your agency?

14. How can the public library collaborate with your agency?

15. What do you see as the major barriers facing libraries in trying to expand their services to meet the needs of at-risk youth?

16. Can you suggest three individuals or agencies who you feel should be contacted for their expertise in working with youth at risk?

This completes the interview. Thank you for your participation.

Sample Focus Group Discussion
Guidelines, Questions, Issues

CITY OF BERKELEY
YOUTH FORUM
GUIDELINES FOR FACILITATORS

This guide supplements the Youth Forum agenda and is intended to help the working group facilitators manage the discussions.

In part I of the agenda, **Welcome/Introduction**, the Mayor or a City Council member will welcome forum participants, introduce other officials present and provide a brief explanation of why the City is sponsoring the Youth Forums. The Mayor will then introduce the meeting facilitator who will provide an overview of the agenda.

Estimated time: 15 minutes (3:05-3:20, 10:05-10:20)

In part II of the agenda, **Issues Facing Berkeley Youth**, the meeting facilitator will introduce the topics for the working groups, mention some examples of issues for each one. Participants will be asked to indicate which group they are most interested in, and adjustments will be made if the groups are unbalanced. Participants will then be assigned to a working group. The topics are:

- Transportation
- Housing/Neighborhoods
- Information/Communication
- Teen Places/Hang-outs
- Marketplaces/Shopping
- Schools
- Libraries
- Parks/Open Space
- Workplaces/Employment
- Health Care

Estimated time: 20 minutes (3:20-3:40, 10:20-10:40)

In part III, Forum Working Groups, participants will adjourn to their assigned groups, each with an adult and a youth facilitator. Working groups will proceed according to the following outline:

A.   Welcome/Introduction by the Facilitators.

B.   Small Group Process

1. **Vision of Berkeley**

Participants will be asked to envision and draw one element that would improve their topic area for youth, ie. the Transportation group will be asked to envision a mode of transportation that could be added or improved. This could include everything from bikeways to better design of streets.   After 10 minutes of quiet time, the facilitator will ask each participant to introduce themselves and briefly describe the vision, recording important points and elements. The facilitator will also ask for a volunteer to serve as a reporter back to the whole group.

Estimated time: 20 minutes (3:40-4:00, 10:40-11:00)

2.   **Define issues**

The facilitator will review the issues as they have been defined and ask participants to reflect on the topic and list other issues not yet identified. This is not an in-depth discussion of each issue, just a list of those issues related to the topic. The facilitator will record each issue as it is named, encouraging new ideas or items not previously mentioned (in order to avoid repetition). The facilitator should call on each person in turn. Rephrase or restate the comments to emphasize to participants that their comments have been received.

Estimated time: 15 minutes (4:00-4:15, 11:00-11:15)

3.   **Prioritize issues**

The facilitator will read the list of all of the issues identified, and ask participants to think about the three most important. The group will come to a consensus about the three most important issues.

Estimated time: 10 minutes (4:15-4:25, 11:15-11:25)

4. Develop issues

The facilitator will state one of the priority issues and ask participants to elaborate on the issue. The facilitator will encourage participants to be specific when describing the issue. When the issue has been developed, the facilitator will bring up the next priority issue. The faciliator should call on each person in turn and record and rephrase comments to emphasize to participants that their concerns have been received.

Estimated time: 20 minutes (4:25-4:45, 11:25-11:45)

·FIVE MINUTE BREAK

5. Formulate action steps

The facilitator will reconvene the group, distribute index cards, and ask participants to write down ideas for specific action steps for each of the three priority issues. Beginning with the first issue, the facilitator will ask for all ideas, regardless of feasability or cost. The facilitator will do this for each issue, recording comments.

Estimated time: 15 minutes (4:50-5:05, 11:50-12:05)

6. Prioritize action steps

The facilitator will return to the action steps for each issue and have the participants identify the top priority. The participants will develop each action in depth, with the facilitator recording comments.

Estimated time: 20 minutes (5:05-5:25, 12:05-12:25)

The facilitator will then summarize the group's work, confirming highlights and main findings for presentation to the whole forum by the volunteer.

In part IV of the agenda, **Working Groups Report to Full Forum**, the meeting facilitator will reconvene the full forum for a report by each working group. Facilitators should assist in the reporting back sessions by queuing up wall graphics or flip chart stands, and prompting the reporters if necessary. Each working group will have 3 minutes to report on priority issues and strategies. These comments will be recorded on a large wall graphic.

Estimated time: 30 minutes (5:25-5:55, 12:25-12:55)

In part V of the agenda, Wrap-Up and Next Steps, the meeting facilitator will briefly summarize the results of the youth forums, and explain that the results will appear in a summary report to be presented to the City Council. The Mayor or a City Council member will then thank participants for participating and close the youth forums.

Estimated time: 5 minutes (5:55-6:00, 12:55-1:00)

BERKELEY YOUTH FORUM
Working Group Issues

LIBRARIES

Libraries are a valuable resource in the community.

1. How can the function of libraries be expanded? What other services should they offer?

2. How can the environment of the library be redesigned for comfort and these new uses?

3. How can the library serve multicultural needs?

4. How can youth get involved in the library?

Focus Group Discussion Questions

Alameda Free Library

1. What are the major problems teens face?

2. What concerns *you* personally?

3. What information do teens need?

4. What would get you to come to the library?

5. What activities/information would you like to see at the library?

Optional:

6. What activities/information would you like to see the library offer at other locations?

Where should these activities/information programs be offered?

(Shopping malls, rec centers, neighborhood centers, school sites, public housing sites, drug/alcohol treatment facilities, fast food restaurants, other)

Sample Key Informant Interviews

San Francisco Public Library

Key Informant Interviews

Hon. Tom Ammiano, San Francisco Board of Education

Charlene Clemens, Teenage Parent Program

Carlos Garcia, Horace Mann Middle School

James Loyce, Juvenile Justice Commission

Joseph Lum, Chinatown Youth Agency

Ruth Passen, Potrero Hill Neighborhood House

Janet Shalwitz, M.D., Department of Public Health, Youth Guidance Center

Vu Duc Vuong and Loc Wagner, Center for Southeast Asian Refugee Resettlement

Nancy Walker, Former San Francisco Supervisor

Neighborhood Interviews

Bayview/Hunters Point

Darryl Edwards, Bayview/Hunters Point Community Foundation

Dan Kugler, Catholic Charities of San Francisco, Southeast

Bill Marquis, San Francisco Senators

Toye Moses, Young Community Developers

Cheryl Towns, New Bayview Committee

Ruben Smith, Hunters Point Boys Club

Outer Mission

Garry Bieringer, San Francisco Education Services, Aria School

Jay Berlin, Alternative Family Services

Brenda Franklin, Portola Recreation Center

Captain Diarmid Philpott, Juvenile Division, SFPD

Donna Roper, Mission YMCA

Jerome Wysinger, Portola Boys and Girls Club

Tenderloin

Jody Friedman, Hospitality House Youth Program

Keith Grier, Recreation Director, Boedekker Park

Mark Larrocca, Career Resource Development Center

Virginia Shepley, Glide "Computers and You"

Olin Simon, Tenderloin YMCA

Midge Wilson, Bay Area Women's Resource Center

Brenda Wong, Tenderloin Youth Center

Sample Research Design Outline

**Research Design
Outline for
Bay Area Youth
at Risk Project**

I. **PROVIDER SURVEY**

Goal: To assess the opinions of youth service
providers — administrators, planners,
youth workers — on the needs of youth at
risk in the communities in which they work

Method: Use of mailed, three-page, self-administered
questionnaire, including both open- and
close-ended questions

Sample: Purposive (or random) sample of fifty to sixty
public and non-profit agencies from list of
agencies serving youth ages ten to
eighteen. List will be generated by Bay
Area Information and Retrieval System
(BAIRS) resource directory for each
city/county and supplemented by
  • Local youth services directories
  • Informal service network lists
  • Self-help groups, clubs, etc.
  • Unified School District employee lists

Key Variables:

A) Demographics/ID
      (1) Name of agency
      (2) Name and position of respondent
      (3) Years in youth services
      (4) Primary population served

B) "Most serious problems facing youth": (top three)

C) "Most serious youth needs in your community":
ranked order (top five)

D) Suggested library programs "which could respond to
need": (open-ended)

E) "Underserved groups of youth":
      (1) Age
      (2) Ethnicity
      (3) Gender
      (4) Neighborhood
      (5) Immigrant/refugee/language

F) "Library services for youth in need of development"

G) "Most useful library services for youth-serving agencies"

Follow-up: At least one call back will be made to agency
director as needed to increase return rate

Individual/Organization Responsible:
      Research Consultant

II. SECONDARY DATA

Goal: To assemble key demographics and socioeconomic and health data on youth in city/county, to provide objective measures of youth need

Method: Utilize all available data from both public documents and existing reports, studies, etc., describing youth demographics and problems in each site, including:
- Census (Donnelly Demographics, ABAG, etc.)
- Vital statistics (Health Department)
- School performance (School District)
- Special reports
- Etc.

Key Indicators: (see attached list)

Individual/Organization Responsible:
Research Consultant

III. INTERVIEWS (Key Informants)

Goal: To assess opinions of key informants (adults and youth) in each city/county about the needs of youth and the ability of library services to respond to those needs

Method: Conduct telephone and/or face-to-face interviews with selected sample of key respondents utilizing a semi-structured schedule of questions, with the use of probes as needed

Sample: Develop purposive sample (household survey, n=30) from list of key community leaders, including:
- Youth-service providers
- Elected officials
- Generalist planners and program staff
- Youth leaders
- Civic leaders (e.g., United Way, ethnic organizations, neighborhood clubs, etc.)
- School officials (principals, counselors, teachers, PTA members, etc.)

Key Variables:
- Needs of high-risk youth by age, ethnicity, neighborhood, etc.
- Major gaps in services for youth
- Ideas on improving library services to youth
- Library services in greatest need (by youth, and by youth-serving agencies)
- Current image of library services for youth
- Suggestions for collaborative projects involving librarians and youth-serving agencies
- Suggestions for funding innovative library services

IV. GROUP INTERVIEWS (Focus Groups)

Goal: To assess opinions of interested citizens (adults and youth) in group discussion setting

Method: Assemble two to three groups of five to twenty-five adults and/or youth and engage in a one to two hour, semi-structured, interactive conversation on the needs of youth and the role that public libraries can play in each community or neighborhood to address those needs. A skilled facilitator will lead each group, and a recorder will be available to take notes on discussion. Both question/answer and brainstorming techniques will be utilized.

Sample: Select purposive sample of key informants from several sources *or* attend planned meeting of existing group (classroom, neighborhood council or board meeting) and conduct focus group session

Variables: (all relevant issues—see attached facilitator's guide)

Individual/Organization Responsible:
Research Consultant

Sample Youth at Risk Service Plan Proposal

San Francisco Public Library

YOUTH-AT-RISK PROGRAM PROPOSAL

Written by: Laura Lent

Youth-at-Risk Planning Committee Members:
  Rosalind Chang
  Loretta Dowell
  Lee Olivier
  Neel Parikh
  Kay Roberts
  Grace Ruth
  Marilyn Smulyan
  Shelley Sorenson
  Thomas Tavis

September 26, 1991

The Youth-at-Risk Project is an LSCA Project funded by the
California State Library

INTRODUCTION

San Francisco Public Library's Youth-at-Risk Program Proposal results from a collaborative process that involved the efforts of several committees as well as dozens of individuals and organizations. The goal of the process is to expand and improve public library services for youth-at-risk. Nine Bay Area library systems have participated in the project, sponsored by the Bay Area Library and Information System (BALIS) and funded by a grant from the California State Library through a Library Services and Construction Act (LSCA) grant. The service plan is the culmination of a one-year planning process; as the project continues into its second year the participating systems will begin to implement their recommendations.

We are indebted to the work of Stan Weisner, project director, who in addition to coordinating the Bay Area Youth-at-Risk Project as a whole and attending many of San Francisco's committee meetings, organized four innovative and highly successful workshops that allowed the staffs of the nine library systems to receive joint training and share ideas as they developed their service plans.

We are also indebted to Marilyn Smulyan, who conducted the San Francisco needs assessment. By examining with an independent eye the juncture of libraries and the needs of at-risk youth she made an invaluable contribution to our project. She was assisted in her task by Sarah Wilcox, demographer Mollie Ward, and CAL Associates, who conducted a written survey about the needs of youth-at-risk. The needs assessment incorporates current demographic information with the knowledge and insights of youth service providers and youth to bring us a unique body of information about the needs of youth and how the library can best meet them.

Finally, we want to thank those who served on the 15-member Youth-at-Risk Planning Team (see appendix). Composed of eight librarians, a library commissioner, a representative of the mayor's office, four youth service agency professionals and a youth representative, this group met three times and contributed greatly to shaping the direction of the needs assessment and recommendations. The Youth-at-Risk Planning Committee, convened by Chief of Branches Neel Parikh, then worked with recommendations from the needs assessment and from the Youth-at-Risk Planning Team and takes final responsibility for this program proposal.

Executive Summary

The mission of our service plan is to develop strategies to better serve youth-at-risk at San Francisco libraries. Our needs assessment shows that San Francisco's young adult population is more likely to live in poverty than the general population of San Francisco. They are also more likely to face problems of discrimination and newcomer adjustment. While 47% of the total population of San Francisco are non-Hispanic whites, the population of those aged 17 and under reflects a greater diversity; 74.6% are Asians, Pacific Islanders, African Americans, Hispanics or from other non-white groups. Of the difficulties that youth face, poverty, educational and health related problems are the most serious. As a result of our needs assessment process we realized that the Library can make the largest and most effective contribution by addressing educational and information needs.

Status indicators and the survey results in our needs assessment show that African American youth, particularly males, are most at risk, followed by Latino youth and those with limited English proficiency. This information shaped our selection of three neighborhoods -- Bayview/ Hunters Point, the Outer Mission, and the Excelsior --for more intensive study. In addition, we want to focus neighborhood based efforts on middle-school aged youth. This approach builds on the strengths of existing Children's Services and in our view has the highest likelihood of success.

Designing new services for youth-at-risk and encouraging experimentation in the delivery of those services will enable us to develop the most successful possible models for serving all of San Francisco's youth, a majority of whom are at risk in one or more of the following ways -- at risk of school failure, poor health outcomes, racial discrimination, family disfunctioning, delinquency, or poverty and unemployment.

The San Francisco Public Library will begin to expand and improve its services to young adults by evaluating our rules, policies and procedures with the goal of reducing barriers that prevent or discourage youth from using the library. We will implement two pilot projects of focused services to youth-at-risk. Targeted services at the Bayview/Anna E.

-2-

Waden Branch Library will include a teen alcove with an expanded special collection, and cooperative projects with local agencies and schools. We will also implement a pilot project for off-site library services at San Francisco's Youth Guidance Center. Finally, we will apply the successes of the pilot projects to other branches, and conduct a citywide publicity campaign promoting use of the library by youth.

Utilizing existing resources and a pilot project grant from the State Library, the San Francisco Public Library will implement the pilot projects and the review of rules, policies and procedures during the current fiscal year. The Youth-at-Risk Committee will also create a budget proposal that would allow for expansion of the targeted services to other branches. In 1992-93 we will conduct a citywide multimedia publicity campaign advertising our expanded services for young adults and promoting the use of the library by youth.

The effectiveness of changes made in policies and procedures will be judged by the extent of increased participation of the target audience in library activities over a two-year period after their implementation. Measures will include circulation statistics for young adult collections, young adult visits to the library, attendance at programs for young adults and evaluations by staff and community agencies working with the target group. The success of the pilot programs at the the Bayview/Anna E. Waden Branch and the Youth Guidance Center will be judged by traditional library measurements such as registration and circulation statistics. At the Youth Guidance Center we will also conduct follow-up surveys of the participants in the program and the probationary department staff. San Francisco Public Library will thereafter continue the pilot programs and incorporate their successes into its service plan for all young adults.

-3-

NEEDS STATEMENT

For this project, we defined at-risk youth as those between the ages of 12 and 18 , who are at risk of school failure, poor health outcomes, racial discrimination, family disfunctioning, delinquency, or poverty and unemployment. Our needs assessment, conducted in the spring and summer of 1991, dramatically documents the needs and problems of San Francisco youth. These needs were documented statistically through demographic information and other measures of the status of youth, through surveys and interviews of youth service providers, and by convening focus groups of youth in targeted neighborhoods.

We discovered a San Francisco in which a relatively small percentage of households (21%) include children under the age of 18. The adolescent population is estimated to number about 35,000. While household incomes in San Francisco have doubled in the last ten years, there is evidence that many families with children have not shared proportionately in this increase. In 1990, 19% of San Francisco's children were AFDC recipients, a rise from 15% in 1980. Families headed by a single parent made up 29 percent of the total number of families in 1980 (the 1990 census figures are not yet available in this category). There are now an estimated 1500 children in homeless families. In addition, San Francisco hosts a large population of unaccompanied homeless youth; almost 1400 were served by the San Francisco Homeless Youth Network in 1989-90.

Our needs assessment shows an alarming level of risk in the areas of health care and health-related problems for San Francisco youth. Child hospitalization statistics show that over half (54%) of children hospitalized in 1986 and 1987 were either uninsured or Medi-Cal insured. More than 90% of reported cases of gonorrhea in San Francisco occur among teens aged 15-19, and the rates of gonorrhea here are ten times higher than the national average. The incidence of syphilis in the 15-19 year age group has nearly doubled in the past three years and is three times higher than the national average.

San Francisco has the highest density of AIDS cases in the nation. While relatively few cases have been reported among children and teens, through May of 1991 there have been 1299 cases reported among 20-29 year olds,

-4-

and it is highly probable in these cases that HIV was contracted during the teen years. According to data from the National Invitational Conference on AIDS in Adolescents, one-third of San Francisco's adolescent population is at high risk for this life-threatening disease. These high risk adolescents are likely to come from inner city neighborhoods, often ethnic minority neighborhoods, with a high rate of drug use and a high rate of sexually transmitted diseases. It is especially interesting to note the characteristics listed by this report for high risk adolescents: 1/poor skills and school performance, dropping out 2/ youth detained in correctional facilities 3/sexual minority youth (estimated to be about 10% of the adolescent population) 4/ drug and alcohol abuse 5/ early pregnancy 6/ youth involved in prostitution for money or drugs and 7/ chronic joblessness.

Through public and private school enrollment statistics, we saw that students are more ethnically and lingually diverse than the general population and therefore more likely to have problems with discrimination and newcomer adaptation issues. About 86% of public school enrollees are from minority groups; 28% have limited English proficiency. According to school district officials, two out of three students go home after school and speak another language. Over half (52.4%) are considered "educationally disadvantaged," meaning that they have scored below the 40th percentile in reading and/or math of the California Test of Basic Skills. The three year dropout rate for the district was 17.7% (1989-90 figure); the highest rates were for African American (28%) and Spanish-surnamed (27%) youth.

The Library's Youth-at-Risk Planning Team examined this information in light of the greatest needs of youth as described in the key informant survey of youth service providers. Respondents identified family problems, literacy level, and drugs and alcohol as the top three problems for teens between 12 and 14. For teens between 15 and 18 drugs and alcohol ranked as the number one problem followed by family problems and dropping out of school.

Our team then examined these needs to see what role the library could most effectively play in addressing the problems of youth. We decided that, of the most critical needs of youth identified, the Library's

-5-

strengths would be best used in addressing the educational and informational needs of youth-at-risk. Based on the preliminary demographic results, we decided that the remainder of the needs assessment process should focus on African American and Latino youth and on communities where there is a high degree of limited English proficiency. The particular neighborhoods that we chose -- Bayview/ Hunters Point, the Excelsior and the Tenderloin -- met these criteria and have existing library facilities that can serve as bases for additional youth services. We agree with the results of our needs assessment showing that the library has the most potential to be successful in serving the younger youth-at-risk population, 12-14 years old or roughly corresponding to middle-school age.

We also decided to target the Youth Guidance Center as a potential site for a depository library program. Our needs assessment shows that the Outer Mission and Bayview/Hunters Point -- the two neighborhoods that together form the southeast quadrant of the City and correspond with our study area for increased branch services--are the two neighborhoods with the most youth referrals for law violations. The majority of referrals are African American youth (53.6%), followed by white youth (17.6%) and Latino youth (12.3%). Males account for 83.2% of all law violations. Most of the juveniles (79%) have had prior contact with the detention system. In 1990, the average stay at the Youth Guidance Center was eleven days; the average population 109. While youth incarcerated at the Youth Guidance Center attend school at the Woodside Learning Center and have textbooks, they have not had access to library facilities. The staff have expressed enthusiasm for the idea of a depository collection, and space is available.

While we estimate that 20-25% of San Francisco library patrons fall into the 12-18 age range, traditionally library services for children and for adults have been emphasized over services for the young adult age group. Recognition of the need for more specifically-tailored services to the young adult age group has been a national trend in library services in recent years, and many library systems have created young adult departments and support specialized staff to meet the needs of this age group. The need for increased services to children and youth was recently reinforced by the vote of the delegates to the White House Conference on

-6-

Library and Information Services, who made services to youth their top recommended priority.

In San Francisco, branch libraries purchase and maintain small collections, mostly paperbacks, of young adult books. Planning for the new Main Library has provided an impetus for the library to evaluate its services to young adults. The new Main plans include a young adult area which will be staffed by young adult specialists. The 1540 square foot area includes 24 reader seats and can accomodate a collection of 5, 000 circulating books and 600 reference titles, as well as 30 periodical titles and 200 audiovisual items.

Last year the library made a commitment to the development of young adult library services. A Young Adult Planning Committee was formed. This committee is evaluating the scope of young adult services and developing a plan for serving young adults throughout the San Francisco Public Library system. In addition, we have taken advantage of the opportunity afforded us by the the Youth-at-Risk grant to make specific plans for serving an important sector of San Francisco's young adult population. Our final service plan for young adults will benefit from the experience gained through our youth-at-risk planning process and pilot projects.

-7-

MISSION

The mission for the San Francisco Public Library is:

To be the focal institution for publicly supported access to information, knowledge and reading in San Francisco. Special emphasis is placed upon meeting the needs of San Francisco's culturally diverse, and multi-lingual community, utilizing the most up-to-date technologies available.

In addition, last year the Young Adult Planning Committee drafted a Young Adult Services Mission:

San Francisco Public Library's Young Adult services mission is to provide and promote library services and materials relevant to the unique recreational and informational needs of the city's diverse adolescent population, aged 13-18, supporting their transition from childhood into adulthood, and encouraging their lifelong use of libraries.

It is our contention that by designing services to meet the needs of at-risk youth we can better achieve San Francisco Public Library's mission. The mission of our Program Proposal is to develop strategies to better serve youth-at-risk at San Francisco libraries. Designing services to meet the needs of our most vulnerable youth population will help us to develop an overall young adult service plan sensitive to those who are most at risk.

-8-

SAN FRANCISCO PUBLIC LIBRARY YOUTH-AT-RISK PROJECT
GOALS AND OBJECTIVES

To achieve our mission we have outlined the following goals and objectives:

1/ GOAL: Revise current library policies, services and procedures to remove barriers to serving youth at risk.

OBJECTIVES:

 · By June 1992 the Youth-at-Risk Planning Committee will evaluate financial obstacles to library use and recommend changes in fee policies to the Library's Administrative Team.
- Identify library fees that have an impact on youth use
- Consider raising the age level for fine immunity higher than the current ceiling of twelve years old
- Consider the lowering or elimination of fine and fee debts through an amnesty program, and/or a work program to help young adults pay their fines and material replacement fees

 · By June 1992 the Youth-at-Risk Planning Committee will evaluate rule and policy barriers to the use of the library by youth and make recommendations for changes to the Library's Administrative Team.
- Examine noise and food policies in respect to young adult preferences to be able to make more noise, eat and drink while using the library
- Examine hours of operation in light of youth needs
- Consider converting some library meeting rooms to supervised young adult areas where existing rules can be relaxed

 · By June 1992 the Youth-at-Risk Planning Committee will recommend to the Library's Administrative Team methods of publicity to maximize youth awareness of adopted changes. The publicity program will be implemented by the Community Relations Librarian.

-9-

2/ GOAL: To develop a model for focused library services for youth-at-risk at branch libraries, working in partnership with community agencies and schools.

OBJECTIVES:

· By March 1992, librarians at the Bayview/Anna E. Waden Branch Library will establish a teen corner and build an expanded collection for Bayview/Hunters Point youth.
- Furnish the alcove area designated for the collection
- Decorate and design appropriate signage
- In consultation with teens from the community, build an expanded collection that includes books, periodicals and audiocassettes
- Organize a reception for the opening

· By October 1992, librarians at the Bayview/Anna E. Waden Branch Library will work with Bayview/Hunters Point Youth Services, other agencies and schools to develop at least three cooperative ventures.
- Compile a list of all youth-serving agencies and schools in the community
- Select agencies and schools with the most potential for collaboration
- Meet with staff of selected youth-serving community agencies and schools
- Identify areas of common concern
- Develop cooperative projects with three of the agencies or schools

· By June 1992, librarians at the Bayview/Anna E. Waden Branch Library will explore ways of opening the community room for individual youth or in cooperation with community agencies.
- Assess community interest in the idea
- Find a method to supervise the room using volunteers or the staff of community agencies
- Establish policies, rules and hours of operation for young adult use of the community room

-10-

· By January 1992 the Youth-at-Risk Planning Committee will complete an assessment of the current organization of Young Adult Services at the Main Library.

    - In cooperation with Children's Department staff, consider incorporating the Young Adult collection into the Children's Room

    - If that is not possible, consider improvements in the placement of the collection in the Information Services/ Circulating Library Department

    - Consider changing the name of the collection as suggested by the needs assessment

· By March 1992, the Youth-at-Risk and Young Adult Planning Committees will develop a budget proposal for young adult and youth-at-risk services systemwide.

    - Give special consideration to developing targeted services for the Tenderloin and Outer Mission neighborhoods

    - Present proposals to the Library's Administrative Team to incorporate into the fiscal year 1992-93 library budget

    - If the Children's Amendment shall pass, present a proposal to the Administrative Team to incorporate into the Children's Amendment budget

3/ GOAL: To create a model for providing off-site services designed to reach youth-at-risk.

OBJECTIVES:

· Working with the Youth-at-Risk Planning Committee and the Youth Guidance Center staff, a librarian assigned to the project will develop policies, procedures and services for an off-site library program to commence in March 1992 at the Youth Guidance Center.

· By January 1992, the librarian will create a mechanism for youth involvement in the Youth Guidance Center project.

-11-

· By March 1992, the librarian will orient Youth Guidance Center staff and the teachers at Woodside Learning Center to on-site and citywide library services.

· If the Children's Amendment shall pass, the Youth-at-Risk Planning Committee will present a budget proposal to the Library's Administrative Team to incorporate into the Children's Amendment budget.

4/ GOAL: To create a targeted publicity campaign to promote library use by youth-at-risk.

OBJECTIVES:

· In fiscal year 1992-93, after developing expanded services for Young Adults and Youth-at-Risk citywide, the Library will create a targeted publicity campaign to attract youth to the library.
- Develop a multimedia publicity campaign including radio and television PSAs, posters and flyers
- Create a youth-based outreach program to promote library services to youth in schools

-12-

EVALUATION

Measures used to judge the effectiveness of the pilot programs and changes in policies and procedures will be taken over a two-year period after implementation. Measures will attempt to answer the question "How well are we meeting the educational and informational needs of youth-at-risk?" and will include the following:

1/ To measure the effectiveness of changes in policies and procedures:
- Track circulation statistics for young adult collections
- If possible with our new circulation system, track young adult registrations
- Record the number of youth participating in fine or fee amnesty programs

2/ To measure the effectiveness of the on-site pilot program at the Bayview/Anna E. Waden Branch:
- Take samples semiannually to assess changes in the number of youth using the branch
- Monitor circulation of young adult materials
- If possible, track young adult registrations at the branch
- Track attendance for special events and cooperative ventures that are an outgrowth of the project
- Survey staff of community agencies and schools that have participated in cooperative projects

3/ To measure the effectiveness of the off-site pilot program at the Youth Guidance Center:
- Monitor circulation of materials borrowed at the Youth Guidance Center
- Monitor registration of borrowers
- Determine whether it is possible to measure circulation -- after youths are released --on library cards issued at the Youth Guidance Center
- Survey staff at the Youth Guidance Center and at Woodside Learning Center on a semiannual basis

-13-

NEXT STEPS AND CONTINUATION

The process for approving our program proposal for youth-at-risk includes the following steps 1/ Approval by the Youth-at-Risk Planning Committee 2/ Approval by the Library's Administrative Team and 3/ Approval by the Library Commission.

In the following years the San Francisco Public Library will work toward incorporating the successes of this program into its service plan for young adults.

-14-

Facts about Foundations*

Foundations are nonprofit agencies which have been set up to grant money to charitable organizations. A foundation can be formed by an individual, a group of individuals, or an organization. Although the range of fields of interest is limitless, each foundation has its own set of funding objectives.

There are approximately 23,700 grantmaking and operating foundations in the United States and, currently, 4,402 have assets of $1 million or more, or provide total annual grants of $100,000 or more. Foundation giving represents about six percent of the total philanthropic dollar.

There are certain legal tax provisions which may help a grant-seeker in understanding how foundations operate.

1. Foundations are required to pay out an amount equivalent to five percent of their assets in charitable contributions each fiscal year.

2. Most foundations are endowed. These funds are invested and become the criterion for the five percent donation requirement. Some foundations, most notably corporate ones, are given funds which are distributed in the same year and never become assets. For example, a company may give $500,000 to its foundation which will then distribute all of these funds in the same year.

3. Foundations must pay a two percent excise tax on their investment income which pays for the IRS to enforce the tax statutes affecting them. A recent change in laws affecting foundations allows them to opt for a reduced tax of one percent, with an amount equivalent to the other one percent paid out in grants.

4. Foundations are required to disclose the names of their grant recipients and the amounts given to each. This information can be found on a foundation's annual tax return called the 990 PF.

5. Recipient organizations must be classified by the IRS as within the 501(c)(3) tax exempt status, with rare exceptions.

6. Foundations are restricted in giving to individuals, and they must file special forms with the IRS before they can do so. As a result, few foundations make grants directly to individuals.

TYPES OF FOUNDATIONS

Community Foundations

These foundations are "for, by and of" a specific community. They represent a pool of funds created by many donors instead of a single or limited source. The geographic area of interest is often evident in the title of the foundation.

National Foundations

These foundations are large, generally with broad purposes and likely to give to programs having national impact.

Special Interest Foundations

These foundations restrict their grants to a specific field of interest, often as a result of the terms of a will or their articles of incorporation. They are a good source if your project falls within their area of interest. They are also a good source of "state of the art" information and advice, if you are seeking support in their fields of interest.

Family Foundations

These foundations have been created to facilitate the charitable contributions of a particular family. The family members are the donors and usually sit on the board. Their pattern of giving is often tied directly to the family's interests. Since they are often community based, they may have the ability to be approached on a less formal basis. They are often a good source of general or operating support. An organization may find itself favored by these foundations for several years, if some area of common interest can be developed.

Corporate or Company-Sponsored Foundations

Such foundations derive funds from a donor company or corporation which usually bears the same name. Established by businesses as a means of carrying out systematic programs of charitable giving, they typically focus on the educational, cultural and social welfare needs of communities where the company's plants are found and employees reside. Among many other reasons, these foundations exist to enhance corporate image.

Operating Foundations

A classification for foundations that do not make grants with most of their money but instead operate their own charitable activities and programs.

*From the Nonprofit Development Center, San Jose, California

APPENDIX K.

Steering Committee Project Evaluation Indicators

Bay Area Youth at Risk Project Evaluation

Each pilot project will be evaluated to assess the degree to which its goals and objectives were reached. Three or four sites will be studied in greater depth (Alameda County, Berkeley, Richmond, and San Francisco), but each library will be involved in the evaluation process.

Please review the goals and objectives of your YAR plan and develop a list of outcome data which you feel can be collected and measured. These might include:

YA Utilization
- YA library use (e.g., visits, reference requests, etc.)
- Number of YA library cards issued
- Types of materials borrowed
- Ethnic and language diversity of YA users

Special YAR Programs
- Number and frequency of programs
- Number and diversity of participants (age, ethnicity, gender)
- Participant satisfaction (questionnaire/interview)
- Quality of program (participant observation)
- Quality and effectiveness of publicity

Community Outreach
- Number of contacts with youth-serving agencies
- Number of community presentations (schools, agencies, etc.)
- Distribution and use of youth resource guides/directories
- Number of collaborative programs with community agencies
- Use of publicity (flyers, media contacts, etc.)

YA Staffing/Equipment/Space
- Number of YA librarians (FTE)
- Number of YA service support staff (pages, clerks, etc.)
- Square footage devoted to teen rooms
- Teen room ambience (signs, furniture, posters, pillows, etc.)
- Special equipment (earphones, computers, etc.)

YA Collection Development
- Number of YA books
- Number of YA magazines, special catalogues, etc.
- Development of special materials (jobs, sex, drugs, college, etc.)

Community Perception of YA Library Services
- Youth attitude toward library (questionnaire or interview)
- Key informant survey (teachers, agency staff, etc.)

YAR Impact
- School indicators (drop-out rates, test scores, etc.)
- Social agency assessment (juvenile hall, tutoring programs, youth employment)

Other
- Name change (e.g., "YA" to "Teen" Services)
- YA rules and regulations changes (fines, eating, music, etc.)
- Use of local media (PSAs, newspaper ads/features, etc.)
- Impact on city/county budget priorities

Training Session Flyers

BAY AREA YOUTH--

"At-Risk" of What? and Why?

A SPECIAL FIRST TRAINING SESSION FOR BAY AREA YOUNG ADULT LIBRARIANS/AND OTHER INTERESTED LIBRARY STAFF

Hosted by the BALIS-Sponsored Bay Area Youth-at-Risk Project

PROGRAM

"Models of Risk-Taking Behavior Among Adolescents"

Jenny Broering, M.S., C.P.N.P.
Associate Clinical Professor
Division of Adolescent Medicine, UCSF

PLUS!

"Communicating with Adolescents--"
A Skills Workshop

Alice Wilkins, LCSW
Berkeley Psychotherapist and Trainer

Thursday, March 28, 1991
8:30 AM - 12:30 PM

The program will be held at West Auditorium, Oakland Public Library located at 125 - 14th Street. Refreshments will be served at 8:30 and the workshops will begin promptly at 9:00.

Registration fees are: **$5.00** for all Participants

Advance registration is required. Please note there will be <u>no refunds</u> of registration fees. For more information/or to register by phone contact Jessi Bowen, at (415) 839-6001.

BAY AREA YOUTH-AT-RISK   Registration is limited/register ASAP

Attention BALIS Library Staff!

NAME_____

If your Library is paying your fee, do not send a check to BALIS. Instead, give this form to your supervisor.

LIBRARY_____

****
The Project Bay Area Youth-at-Risk is Funded
by the California State Library
through the Library Services and Construction Act

MEMBER LIBRARIES: ALAMEDA FREE LIBRARY (CITY); ALAMEDA COUNTY LIBRARY; BERKELEY PUBLIC LIBRARY; CONTRA COSTA COUNTY LIBRARY; HAYWARD PUBLIC LIBRARY; LIVERMORE PUBLIC LIBRARY; OAKLAND PUBLIC LIBRARY; RICHMOND PUBLIC LIBRARY; SAN FRANCISCO PUBLIC LIBRARY.

THE YOUTH SERVING NETWORK
POLITICS AND PROGRAMS

A Training Session for Bay Area Young Adult
Librarians and Other Interested Library Staff

Hosted by the BALIS-Sponsored Bay Area Youth-at-Risk Project

PROGRAM:

Panel One — An Overview of Youth Services

"Statewide Issues - The Range of Services and Models of Collaboration"
Marilyn Eriksen, Executive Director
California Children, Youth and Family Coalition

········

"The Funding and Organization of Social Services to Youth"
Dr. Paul Terrell
School of Social Welfare, U.C. Berkeley

········

"The Status of Adolescent Health and Mental Health Services"
Barbara Staggers, M.D.
Children's Hospital (Oakland)

········

"Falling Through the Cracks - Why Some Youth Don't Make It"
Michelle Magee, Associate Director
Youth Advocates (San Francisco)

Panel Two — Youth Resources Workshops*

1. Youth Employment
2. Tutoring/Mentoring
3. Teen Pregnancy
4. Recreation/After School Programs
5. Social Services
6. Mental Health/Substance Abuse

Thursday, April 18, 1991
8:30 AM - 12:30 PM

The program will be held at West Auditorium, Oakland Public Library
located at 125 - 14th Street. Refreshments will be served at 8:30 and
the workshops will begin promptly at 9:00.

Registration fees are: $5.00 for all Participants
Advance registration is required. Please note there will be <u>no refunds</u> of registration fees. For more
information/or to register by phone contact Jessi Bowen, at (415) 839-6001.

BAY AREA YOUTH-AT-RISK   Registration is limited/register ASAP

LIBRARIANS:
"WHAT HAVE YOU DONE FOR ME LATELY!"
A YOUTH SPEAKOUT

A Training Session for Bay Area Young Adult Librarians
and Other Interested Library Staff

Hosted by the BALIS-Sponsored Bay Area Youth-At-Risk Project

A panel of representative youths from Bay Area cities will present their views of growing up in urban America. This sure to be provocative presentation will offer librarians new insights into how to better shape library services for young adults in the 1990's.

The panel will be convened by Sandy Close *from the Pacific News Service in San Francisco. The session will be taped for cable television (KTOP).*

Thursday, May 16, 1991
8:30 AM - 12:30 PM

The program will be held at West Auditorium, Oakland Public Library located at 125 - 14th Street. Refreshments will be served at 8:30 and the workshop will begin promptly at 9:00.

Registration fee: **$5.00 for all participants**

Advance registration is required. Please note there will be <u>no refunds</u> of registration fees. For more information or to register by phone contact Jessi Bowen at (415) 839-6001.

LIBRARIANS: "WHAT HAVE YOU DONE FOR ME LATELY!"

REGISTRATION DEADLINE IS MAY 9, 1991.

Attention BALIS Library Staff!
If your library is paying your fee, do not send a check
to BALIS. Instead, give this form to your supervisor.

Name_____

The Bay Area Youth at Risk Project is funded by the California State Library through the Library Services & Construction Act

Library_____

Make check payable to BALIS.
Please send this form with your check to BALIS, 520 Third Street, Suite 202, Oakland 94607-3520
MEMBER LIBRARIES: ALAMEDA FREE LIBRARY (CITY); ALAMEDA COUNTY LIBRARY; BERKELEY PUBLIC LIBRARY; CONTRA COSTA COUNTY LIBRARY; HAYWARD PUBLIC LIBRARY; LIVERMORE PUBLIC LIBRARY; OAKLAND PUBLIC LIBRARY; RICHMOND PUBLIC LIBRARY; SAN FRANCISCO PUBLIC LIBRARY

CROSS-CULTURAL ISSUES AND YOUTH

A Training Session for Bay Area Young Adult Librarians
and Other Interested Library Staff

Hosted by the BALIS-Sponsored Bay Area Youth-At-Risk Project

Featuring **Dr. Jewelle Taylor-Gibbs**, author of <u>Young,
Black</u> and <u>Male</u> in <u>America</u> - <u>An Endangered Species</u>
and **Martin Cano** from World of Difference.

*In this workshop Professor Taylor-Gibbs, U.C. Berkeley, School of Social
Welfare, will speak on the topic of African American Youth-At-Risk. Her
presentation will be followed by an interactive workshop on cross-cultural
issues which will be facilitated by Martin Cano.*

Thursday, May 30, 1991
8:30 AM - 12:30 PM

The program will be held at West Auditorium, Oakland Public Library
located at 125 - 14th Street. Refreshments will be served at 8:30 and
the workshop will begin promptly at 9:00.

Registration fee: $5.00 for all participants

Advance registration is required. Please note there will be <u>no refunds</u> of registration fees. For more
information or to register by phone contact Jessi Bowen at (415) 839-6001.

CROSS-CULTURAL ISSUES AND YOUTH

REGISTRATION DEADLINE IS MAY 23, 1991.

Attention BALIS Library Staff!
If your library is paying your fee, do not send a check
to BALIS. Instead, give this form to your supervisor.

Name_____

The Bay Area Youth at Risk Project is
funded by the California State Library
through the Library Services & Construction Act

Library_____

Make check payable to BALIS.
Please send this form with your check to BALIS, 520 Third Street, Suite 202, Oakland 94607-3520
MEMBER LIBRARIES: ALAMEDA FREE LIBRARY (CITY); ALAMEDA COUNTY LIBRARY; BERKELEY PUBLIC LIBRARY; CONTRA COSTA COUNTY LIBRARY;
HAYWARD PUBLIC LIBRARY; LIVERMORE PUBLIC LIBRARY; OAKLAND PUBLIC LIBRARY; RICHMOND PUBLIC LIBRARY; SAN FRANCISCO PUBLIC LIBRARY

Bay Area Youth at Risk Project

WORKSHOP #5
BAY AREA YOUTH-AT-RISK PROJECT

"TURNING THE CORNER" FOR YOUTH-AT-RISK

IMPLEMENTING YOUNG ADULT SERVICES
IN PUBLIC LIBRARIES

PROGRAM:

    OPENING ADDRESS:

        CALIFORNIA: THE STATE OF OUR CHILDREN, 1991

        James Steyer, President, Children Now

    GENERAL SESSIONS/WORKSHOPS (Facilitated by Marilyn Snider)

        Responding to the Needs of At-Risk Youth - A Panel Discussion

        *Developing Effective Strategies for Implementing and
Evaluating Young Adult Services - Workshops*

Wednesday, September 4, 1991
8:30 A.M. - 12:30 p.m.

AT

ALAMEDA COUNTY LIBRARY (FREMONT - MAIN BRANCH "over for map")

The program will include small-group team workshops across library systems, as well as general sessions to share ideas and conduct training exercises.

Registration 8:30 -Workshop begins promptly at 9:00

YAR Workshop #5, Wednesday, September 4, 1991 Cost for all participants - $5.00 (no refunds)

Registration Deadline, August 26, 1991

Attention BALIS Library Staff!
If your library is paying your fee, do not send a check
to BALIS. Instead, give this form to your supervisor.

Name_____

The Bay Area Youth at Risk Project is
funded by the California State Library
through the Library Services & Construction Act

Library_____
Make check payable to BALIS.
Please send this form with your check to BALIS, 520 Third Street, Suite 202, Oakland 94607-3520
MEMBER LIBRARIES: ALAMEDA FREE LIBRARY (CITY); ALAMEDA COUNTY LIBRARY; BERKELEY PUBLIC LIBRARY; CONTRA COSTA COUNTY LIBRARY;
HAYWARD PUBLIC LIBRARY; LIVERMORE PUBLIC LIBRARY; OAKLAND PUBLIC LIBRARY; RICHMOND PUBLIC LIBRARY; SAN FRANCISCO PUBLIC LIBRARY

Young Adult Pamphlet

What's a Y. A.?
Who won the Super Bowl in 1980?
What is the minimum wage for teenagers?
Where are nightclubs for under 18s?
What are the phone numbers for teen crisis information?
How do you spell supercalifragillisticexpialidocious?

A Y.A. is a Young Adult, and that's you if you're between 13 and 19 years old.

The answers to these questions and many more are at your San Lorenzo Public Library, a branch of Alameda County Library, with friendly staff to help you find the answers to your questions. Ask at the Information Desk!

In the Young Adult Area, a special part of the library for teenagers, you'll find:

- paperbacks and hardbacks
- fiction: romance, horror, science fiction, adventure
- nonfiction: sports, music, drugs, AIDS, coping, biographies, humor, relationships, sex, and more
- magazines: Thrasher, Sassy, Circus Mad and more
- CDs and records: rock, soul, heavy metal, rap, modern rock, soundtracks and more

You'll also find homework help:

Librarians to help you find what you need!
For research, you'll find:
- computerized library catalog with printer
- encyclopedias and reference books
- magazine article indexes
- magazines, newspapers, and microfilm
- pamphlet file

Other resources include:
- Cliffs Notes
- classics
- biographies

In other parts of the library, you'll find:

- job center with interview, resume and career guides
- college catalogs, guides, financial aid and scholarship information
- high school yearbooks
- videos
- CDs
- community resource file
- automobile Blue Books and other consumer resources
- books in Spanish, Chinese, Japanese, Korean, Vietnamese, and ESL materials
- public access computer with software
- display case
- bulletin boards
- meeting room
- typewriter
- copy machine
- public pay phone
- and much more...

Loan Periods

Most books may be borrowed for three weeks. Records, CDs, encyclopedias, and pamphlets may be borrowed for one week. Most videos may be borrowed for two days. There are no fines for overdue materials. If you have materials that are overdue, you may not be able to check out anything until they are returned.

Interlibrary Loans

This is a free service that allows us to borrow books, CDs, and other materials for you from other libraries. Just ask at the Information Desk, in person or by phone.

Other Services

Telephone reference. . .call us for confidential answers to your questions.

Reader's Advisory . . . we'll help you find just the right book.

Special topic programs . . .watch for publicity in your school, your library, and your community.

Youth Advisory Committee. . . a chance for you to give advice and ideas about library services that affect you.

Booktalks (by appointment) . . .we will visit your class or group and present books of special interest.

Class and group visits (by appointment) . . . we will provide an orientation to our many resources when your class or group comes to the library.

For more information, ask a Librarian at the Information Desk or your Young Adult Librarian.

Library Cards . . . are free!

To get a card, you need I.D. with your name and address, such as a driver's license or mail that has been sent to you.

If you only have a student body card, you may check out three items, and we will then mail the card to you as a means of address verification.

If you have no I.D., you may apply for a card, which will be mailed to you; however, no items may be checked out until you receive your card.

If you are under 14, a parent's signature is needed.

If you are under 18 and wish to borrow videos, a form must be signed by a parent.

If you have lost or misplaced your card, let us know immediately . . . remember, you're responsible for what's checked out on your card.

San Lorenzo Public Library's Free Prize Drawing!

(all prizes donated by local merchants listed on reverse)

- 1st Prize - Stereo/CD Boom Box
- 2nd Prize - Personal CD Player
- 3rd Prize - $50.00 Gift Certificate
- many other prizes such as free food, CDs, and movie passes

Name _____

Address _____

Phone _____

Age: (please circle one)

13   14   15   16   17   18   19

School: ☐ Arroyo   ☐ San Lorenzo

☐ Bohannon   ☐ other

☐ not currently enrolled

Do you have an Alameda County Library card?
☐ Yes   ☐ No

To enter, bring this coupon to the Information Desk at the San Lorenzo Public Library. You must be between 13 and 19 years old. Enter by March 31, 1992. Prize drawing will be held in April, 1992. You need not be present to win. Winners will be notified by mail. Limit one entry per person.

Free
Prize
Drawing!
(see other side for details)

Among the many merchants we would like to thank for their generous donations:

- *David D. Bohannon Organization (for the 1st and 2nd prizes!)*
- *Carrows*
- *Classic Burger*
- *Crown Books*
- *Festival Cinema*
- *FRIENDS of the Library, San Lorenzo Area, Inc.*
- *Jack in The Box*
- *Rasputin's*
- *Waldenbooks*
- *Zorba's Delicatessen*
- *and many others*

This project is funded by the California State Library through a Library Services & Construction Act (LSCA) grant, with partial funding by the San Francisco Foundation.

*Alameda County Library Community Relations 9/92
Printed on recycled paper with soy-based ink*

San Lorenzo Public Library
395 Paseo Grande
San Lorenzo, CA 94580
Phone (510) 670-6283
Hours:
Monday & Wednesday ... 10:00 A.M. - 6:00 P.M.
Tuesday & Thursday .... 10:00 A.M. - 9:00 P.M.
Friday & Saturday .... 10:00 A.M. - 5:00 P.M.
Sunday .... Closed

How to get to the library
From Arroyo High School:
Take Grant Ave. to Hesperian Blvd., turn right onto Hesperian Blvd., turn left on Paseo Grande, turn left after fire station into driveway. The library is at far end of the parking lot.

From Bohannon Continuation High School:
Take Bockman Rd. to Hesperian Blvd., turn left on Hesperian Blvd., turn right on Paseo Grande and turn left after fire station into driveway. The library is at far end of the parking lot.

From San Lorenzo High School:
Take East Lewelling Blvd. to Via Granada, turn left on Via Granada, turn right on Paseo Grande and go across overpass. Turn right at bottom of overpass into driveway. The library is at far end of the parking lot.

AC Transit
Bus lines #81, 85, 93 and 97 stop near the corner of Hesperian Blvd. and Paseo Grande, which is a very short walk from the library. Bus fares are $1.00 (ages 17+), $0.85 (ages 5-16). Call AC Transit at 582-3035 for details.

Alameda County Library's Young Adult Services is committed to providing books and other materials for the recreational and personal information needs of young adults.

Other Alameda County Libraries

Castro Valley Library
20055 Redwood Rd. Castro Valley CA 94546
Phone (510) 670-6280
Hours:
Monday & Wednesday... 10:00 A.M. - 9:00 P.M.
Tuesday & Thursday .... 10:00 A.M. - 6:00 P.M.
Friday & Saturday .... 10:00 A.M. - 5:00 P.M.
Sunday .... Closed

Fremont Main Library
2400 Stevenson Boulevard
Fremont, CA 94538
Hours recording 745-1400
General Information 745-1401
Reference 745-1444
     This is the Main Library for the Alameda County Library. Its collections include extensive magazine backfiles and reference resources.

Bookmobile
The Bookmobile stops in the Ashland, Cherryland and Edendale areas. Schedules are available at the Library, or call the Bookmobile office at 745-1477.

Neighboring Library

Hayward Public Library
835 "C" Street Hayward, CA 94541
Phone (510) 293-8685

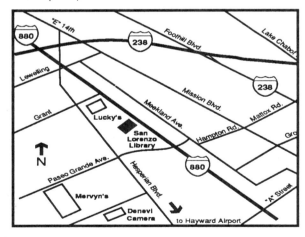

Tutoring Project Publicity

CITY OF OAKLAND

NEWS FROM

THE OAKLAND PUBLIC LIBRARY

For Additional Information:

Kathleen Hirooka,
Community Relations
510/238-6713

FOR IMMEDIATE RELEASE
December 2, 1991

NEW HOMEWORK ASSISTANCE CENTER
TARGETS LOCAL YOUTH-AT-RISK

As part of the Bay Area Youth-at-Risk project, funded by the California State Library, Oakland Public Library is launching a Homework Assistance Center to help tutor students, ages ten through fifteen, at its Martin Luther King, Jr. Branch Library. This center is being jointly sponsored by Oakland School Volunteers and will begin operation December 2, 1991. Its hours will be weekdays, 3:00-5:30 p.m., and Saturdays from 10:00 a.m.-2:00 p.m. Supplemental funds to implement this program have been awarded by the San Francisco Foundation.

The Homework Assistance Center is a response to a community needs assessment funded by the State Library which indicated that school drop-outs and below-grade literacy levels were among the most serious problems faced by teenagers in Oakland. The center will help young adults improve their study skills and master school assignments by providing a quiet study space, resource materials and tutors. The Library is currently recruiting both tutors and students to participate in this program.

Those wishing further information should contact Julie Odofin, Coordinator of Children's Services, (510) 238-3511.

###

Oakland Public Library
Martin L. King Jr. Branch
6833 East 14th Street
Oakland, CA. 94601
(510) 632-4861

HOMEWORK CENTER

Invites persons interested in offering
free homework assistance to Oakland Public
School students grades 5th through 9th to

Volunteer Now

For more information call   MARTIN LUTHER KING JR. BRANCH
LIBRARY at (510) 632-4861

To Volunteer directly call   OAKLAND SCHOOL VOLUNTEERS
(510)   874-5438 AND
REQUEST REGISTRATION MATERIAL

You Can Make a Difference

The Homework center is jointly sponsored by:

Oakland Public Library MLK. Jr. Branch

and

Oakland School   Volunteers
30 Jack London Square
Suite 210
Oakland, CA 94607
(510) 874-5438

This Program is funded by the California State Library through the
Library Services and Construction Act and partially funded by the
San Francisco Foundation.

OAKLAND PUBLIC LIBRARY • 125 - 14TH STREET • OAKLAND, CALIFORNIA 94612
Martin L. King, Jr., Branch   6833 E. 14th Street Oakland

November 1, 1991

Dear Parent or Guardian:

Don't despair! Help is closer than you think! If you have a child
or grandchild between ages 10 and 15, he or she can get free help
in reading, writing, math, social studies and sciences at Oakland
Public Library's new **HOMEWORK CENTER**, opening soon at the Martin
L. King, Jr., Branch, 6833 East 14th Street, Oakland, 94621.

Each child will be matched with a tutor and meet after school
and/or on Saturday mornings at the Homework Center. Please call
632-4861 or come into the King Branch Library to sign up or for
further information.

Space is limited, so sign up soon!

Respectfully,

Garrett Lambrev
Branch Librarian

MARTIN L. KING, JR., BRANCH
of the
OAKLAND PUBLIC LIBRARY

Invites East Oakland Students, 10 to 15 years old,
to sign up for Home Work Help! Help is being offered
EACH DAY at **MARTIN L. KING, JR., BRANCH,**
6833 E. 14th Street.

Space is limited! Sign up now!

To sign up for help, come to or call:
MARTIN L. KING, JR., BRANCH
LIBRARY at (510) 632-4861

YOU CAN MAKE THE GRADE!

The Homework Center is jointly
sponsored by Oakland Public Library
&
Oakland School Volunteers
30 Jack London Square
Suite 210
Oakland, CA 94607
(510) 874-5438

This program is funded by the California State Library
through the Library Services and Construction Act, and
partially supported by the San Francisco Foundation.

162

Press Release and Press Conference Agenda

Bay Area Youth at Risk Project

520 Third Street • Suite 202 • Oakland, CA 94607-3520
Telephone: 415/839-4593 • FAX: 415/834-5193

BAY AREA YOUTH-AT-RISK PROJECT
FUNDED BY THE CALIFORNIA STATE LIBRARY
THROUGH THE LIBRARY SERVICES AND
CONSTRUCTION ACT

ADVISORY COMMITTEE

JOSE ARREDONDO
*Spanish-Speaking
Citizens Foundation*
ANGELA BLACKWELL
Urban Strategies Council
DAVID CARRILLO
*The United Way
(Contra Costa County)*
KEITH CHOY
*Mayor's Office of Children,
Youth and Families (S.F.)*
DEBORAH ELLWOOD
Children Now
EFFIE LEE MORRIS
*California Library
Services Board*
GAIL STEELE
*Eden Youth Center
(Hayward)*
CLAIR STICH
*Bay Area Young Adult
Librarians (BAYA)*
PEDER THOREEN
*Youth Representative,
National White House
Conference on Libraries
and Information Services*
ALAN WATAHARA
*Children and Youth
Policy Project*
PROF. JUDITH WEEDMAN
*School of Library and
Information Studies
(U.C. Berkeley)*
SYLVIA YEE
San Francisco Foundation

LIBRARY STEERING COMMITTEE

STELLA BAKER
Contra Costa County
JULIE CASAMAJOR
Livermore
ADELIA LINES
Richmond
SHERRY KUMLER
Hayward
MARGARET McGOWAN
Alameda City
REGINA MINUDRI
Berkeley
JULIE ODOFIN
Oakland
NEEL PARIKH
San Francisco
CARYN SIPOS
Alameda County
BESSIE EGAN
California State Library

PROJECT DIRECTOR

STAN WEISNER, D.S.W.

SPECIAL EVENT FOR ALL BAYA MEMBERS

PRESS CONFERENCE
Monday, September 30, 1991
9:00 - 11:00 AM
Oakland Public Library, West Auditorium
125 - 14th Street, Oakland

9:00 AM: Welcome/Refreshments
            Martin Gomez, Director, Oakland Public Library

9:15 AM: Address by
            Chris Crutcher, Young Adult Author

10:00 AM: Unveiling Youth-at-Risk Plans

            --Statewide Plans for Youth-at-Risk
                Gary Strong, State Librarian

            --Local Plans for Services
                Stan Weisner, Project Director

                -Alameda City Library
                -Alameda County Library
                -Berkeley Public Library
                -Contra Costa County Library
                -Hayward Public Library
                -Oakland Public Library
                -Livermore Public Library
                -Richmond Public Library
                -San Francisco Public Library

THE BAY AREA YOUTH AT RISK PROJECT IS A PROJECT OF THE
BAY AREA LIBRARY AND INFORMATION SYSTEM

MEMBER LIBRARIES: ALAMEDA FREE LIBRARY (CITY); ALAMEDA COUNTY LIBRARY; BERKELEY PUBLIC LIBRARY; CONTRA COSTA LIBRARY;
HAYWARD PUBLIC LIBRARY; LIVERMORE PUBLIC LIBRARY; OAKLAND PUBLIC LIBRARY; RICHMOND PUBLIC LIBRARY; SAN FRANCISCO PUBLIC LIBRARY.

Bay Area Youth at Risk Project

520 Third Street • Suite 202 • Oakland, CA 94607-3520
Telephone: 415/839-4593 • FAX: 415/834-5193

FOR IMMEDIATE RELEASE
Contact: Stan Weisner, Project Director
             415/839-4593

BAY AREA PUBLIC LIBRARIES IMPLEMENTING NEW STRATEGIES TO SERVE AT-RISK YOUTH

PRESS CONFERENCE: 10:15 AM, Monday, September 30th, 1991
                      Oakland Public Library
                      (West Auditorium - On Madison Street)
                      Main Branch
                      125 14th Street
                      Oakland

Culminating several months of training, coalition-building and needs assessment in the San Francisco Bay Area, nine city and county library systems in Alameda, Contra Costa and San Francisco counties are releasing plans for a range of innovative programs, aimed at improving services to at-risk youth. The public libraries in these counties will be starting-up these programs this fall.

According to Dr. Stan Weisner, Director of the Bay Area Youth-at-Risk Project, "The role of the public library in serving at-risk youth will never be the same again. The Bay Area Youth-at-Risk Project has put teenagers firmly on the agendas of public libraries and, more importantly, has enabled libraries to actively participate in the network of front-line, youth-serving agencies active in developing preventive services to teens in the 1990s."

Gary Strong, the California State Librarian, sees the Bay Area Youth-at-Risk Project as "a replicable state-wide model for planning and expanding young adult services to an emerging generation of youth who are at greater risk than ever before of dropping out of school, substance abuse, teen pregnancy..."

Martin Gomez, Director of the Oakland Public Library, has called the Youth-at-Risk Project "an answer to the question of how we can make the public library more relevant and useful to a whole generation of disaffected youth."

--MORE--

The Youth-at-Risk Project, sponsored by the Bay Area Library and Information System (BALIS), has created a national model for collaborative efforts between public libraries and youth-serving agencies. Programs will include:

* a library outreach "youth corps"
* placement of young adult library services in public housing projects and juvenile halls
* library-sponsored youth forums
* cross-cultural programming
* creation and distribution of a "hip-pocket" youth resource directory
* tutoring volunteer development

The Bay Area Youth-at-Risk Project is funded by the California State Library through the Library Services and Construction Act (LSCA). For further information, call Ruth Foley Metz, BALIS System Coordinator at 839-6001 or Dr. Stan Weisner at 415/839-4593.

# # #

Youth at Risk Panel Presentation Flyer

YOUTH-AT-RISK

UNPEELING THE PLANNING PROCESS FOR YOUNG ADULT SERVICES

BAY AREA YOUTH-AT-RISK PROJECT
FUNDED BY THE CALIFORNIA STATE LIBRARY
THROUGH THE LIBRARY SERVICES AND
CONSTRUCTION ACT

A PANEL DISCUSSION AND VIDEO PRESENTATION

PERSPECTIVES INSIDE AND OUTSIDE THE LIBRARY

SPONSORED BY THE CLA LIBRARY SERVICES DEVELOPMENT AND PLANNING
COMMITTEE, THE CALIFORNIA LIBRARY SERVICES BOARD AND

THE FIFTEEN COOPERATIVE LIBRARY SYSTEMS AND THEIR
ADVISORY BOARDS LOCATED THROUGHOUT THE STATE

Suzanne H. Calpestri, Moderator and Chair, CLA Library Services Development and Planning Committee. Under Ms. Calpestri's leadership, the Committee has been engaged in a two year program to develop a broad base of awareness and support for library services to youth at risk.

Stan Weisner, Ph.D., Project Director, BALIS Youth-at-Risk Project. Dr. Weisner is well known in the Bay Area as an effective advocate for children and youth services. He has been involved in policy and legislative analysis, neighborhood organizing and program development related to children and youth. He is a university lecturer and the recipient of numerous awards for his service on behalf of youth in the Bay Area.

Regina Minudri, Chair, BALIS Youth-at-Risk Steering Committee, Director of Berkeley Public Library and Past President CLA, Past President ALA. She presents the view of a Library Director involved in planning and developing new services for youth at risk.

Ted Bryant, Executive Director, Richmond Boys and Girls Club of America, has spent more than 20 years developing programs for teens throughout the Bay Area. He has conducted both local and national research on work-training, career development and special education and headed a special project for the National Institute of Education on Youth in Transition. Mr. Bryant is a member of the Youth-at-Risk Planning Team in Richmond.

Jane Chisaki, Supervising Librarian for Childrens' Services and Chair of the Youth-at-Risk Planning Team in Alameda. Ms. Chisaki presents perspectives on teens and library services growing out of her extensive work with teens in Sea Scouts and other youth serving agencies. She is the library representative on the Alameda Youth Activities Network.

Amy Vongthavady, DeAnza High School Student and member of the Youth-at-Risk Planning Team in Contra Costa County. Through her own experience and observation she provides insight into why teens do or do not use libraries.

Neel Parikh, Chief of Branch Libraries at San Francisco Public Library and incoming President of CLA. Ms. Parikh brings to the panel expertise from her many years as Children's and Youth Specialist in Bay Area Public Libraries. She is chair of the San Francisco Youth-at-Risk Planning Team.

For further information, please call Stan Weisner, Project Director, BALIS Youth-at-Risk Project at (510) 839-4693 or write to Stan Weisner, c/o BALIS, 530 Third Street, Oakland, CA 94607.

Index